Lanarkshire

Edited by Annabel Cook

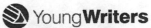 Young**Writers**

First published in Great Britain in 2005 by:
Young Writers
Remus House
Coltsfoot Drive
Peterborough
PE2 9JX
Telephone: 01733 890066
Website: www.youngwriters.co.uk

SB ISBN 1 84602 185 5

Foreword

Young Writers was established in 1991 and has been passionately devoted to the promotion of reading and writing in children and young adults ever since. The quest continues today. Young Writers remains as committed to the fostering of burgeoning poetic and literary talent as ever.

This year's Young Writers competition has proven as vibrant and dynamic as ever and we are delighted to present a showcase of the best poetry from across the UK. Each poem has been carefully selected from a wealth of *Playground Poets* entries before ultimately being published in this, our thirteenth primary school poetry series.

Once again, we have been supremely impressed by the overall high quality of the entries we have received. The imagination, energy and creativity which has gone into each young writer's entry made choosing the best poems a challenging and often difficult but ultimately hugely rewarding task - the general high standard of the work submitted amply vindicating this opportunity to bring their poetry to a larger appreciative audience.

We sincerely hope you are pleased with our final selection and that you will enjoy *Playground Poets Lanarkshire* for many years to come.

Contents

Coalburn Primary School

Kirkshaws Primary School

Jordan Jarvie (8)	34
Sean Gibson (8)	35
Nicole Anderson (8)	35
Ryan Lucas (8)	35
Holly Drummond (8)	36
Claire Marshall (8)	36
Aaron Rae (8)	36
Thomas Young (9)	37
Hannah Grennen (7)	37

Knowetop Primary School

Chloe Craig (11)	37
Marissa Clarke (11)	38
Melissa Dickie (11)	38
Laura Scott (11)	39
Iain Whyte (11)	39
Natalie Anderson (11)	40
Emma Craig (11)	40
Scott Walker Gibson (11)	41
Elliot Baker (11)	42
Lauren Walker (11)	43
Hayley Caldwell (11)	44
Natalie Dunn (11)	45
Lynsey Harris (11)	46
Usman Hussain (11)	47
Megan Hannah (11)	48
Laura McGlashan (11)	49
Debbie Kelly (11)	49
Róisín King (11)	50
Fraser Joyce (11)	51
Rebekah Wilson (11)	51
Susan Cunningham (10)	52
Tommy McGlynn (11)	52
Maria Kennedy (11)	53
Ashley Baird (11)	53
Claire Smith (11)	54
Catriona Walker (11)	55
Heather Patterson (11)	56
Natalie Wallace (11)	56
Jack Cunningham (11)	57

Chloe McMenemy (10)	77
Lee Knox (10)	78
Donnamarie McCusker (10)	78
Rebecca Ryce (10)	79
Fiona Bruce (10)	79
Lynsey McMenemy (10)	80
Amanda Galloway (10)	80
Jennifer Reid (10)	81
Rachael Kelly (10)	82

Our Lady & St Francis Primary School

Amy Townsley (10)	82
Alisha Blair (10)	83
Cheryl Bradley (10)	83
Monica Bonham (11)	84
Stephanie Caldow (9)	85
Nicola Reilly (10)	86
Mobeen Aftab (10)	86
Melissa Austin (10)	86
Katie McShane (10)	87
Joseph Wilson (10)	87
Ryan Clark (10)	87
Kevin Connelly (10)	88
Thomas Sinnott (10)	88
Hayley Morrison (9)	89
John Paul Devlin (10)	89
John Joe Curran (9)	89
Ryan Watson (10)	90
Jennifer Fallon (9)	90
Hayleigh Kemp (9)	91
Nadia Al Murshedy (9)	91
Aimee Crawford (9)	92
Rebecca Hart (9)	92
Daniel Cairney & Christopher Finlay (9)	93
Dean Stewart (10)	93
Nicole Jaques (9)	93
Dylan Baxendale (9)	94
Andrew Miller (9)	94
Conor McCormick (9)	95
Eilish Bennett (8)	95
Megan McLean (8)	95

St Ignatius Primary School, Wishaw

Garry Boyle (10)	96
Megan MacFarlane (10)	96
Paul McConville (10)	97
Gerald McQuade (10)	97
Nicola Rooney (10)	98
Gerard Cassidy (10)	98
Kyle Gray (10)	99
Shane Armstrong (11)	99
Caitlin Glover (10)	100
Andrew Watters (10)	100
Kealan Hughes (9)	100
Barry Hodge (10)	101
Leanne McMillan (10)	101
Liam McQuade (10)	102
Michael Larkin (10)	102
Shannon McNeil (10)	103
Nikita Reilly (10)	103

St Mark's Primary School, Hamilton

Caitlin Leabody (9)	103
Mark Russell (11)	104
Stephen Queen (10)	104
Rebeka Hynes (10)	104
Jenna Dyson (10)	105
Heather McCafferty (9)	105
Lauren Harvey (10)	105
Hayley Simpson (10)	106
Callum Steven (10)	106
Emily Hill (10)	106
Brogan McKendrick (10)	107
Danielle Barr (9)	107
Robert Stone (9)	107
Rachael Feeley (11)	108
Gemma Leabody (8)	108
Sean Leabody (8)	108
Mae Reilly (8)	109
Declan Smith (9)	109
Kieren McCafferty (8)	109
Chloe Stewart (7)	110
Ruairi Fleming (7)	110

Liam Forbes (7)   110
Colin Henderson (7)   111
Jonah Gault (7)   111
Katie Maguire (7)   111
Kerry McGuckin (7)   112
Laura Pollock (8)   112
Kaitlyn Mitchell (7)   112
Nicole Harley (8)   113
Omar Khalaf (8)   113
Lewis Polland (8)   113
Jordan Craig (8)   114
Lyndsey Dyson (8)   114
Jordan Young (8)   114
Kieran Hartley (8)   115
Martin MacPherson (8)   115
Daniel Carlton (7)   115
Declan Doyle (8)   116

St Mary's Primary School, Hamilton

Daniel McRoberts (9)   116
Mark Boyle (8)   116
Megan O'Donnell (8)   117
Jamie Woodward (8)   117
Amy Dougan (8)   117
Scott Agar (8)   118
Ainsley Taylor (8)   118
Lorena Palazzo (8)   118
Matthew Abbott (8)   119
Catriona Cherrie (8)   119
Sarah Duddy (8)   119
Lauren Slaven (8)   120
Dervla McCormick (8)   120
Lewis Kemp (8)   120
Chloe McCluskey (10)   121
Christopher Szafranek (10)   121
Danielle Loughran (10)   122
Vincent Linden (9)   122
Maria Linden (10)   123
Michael Lowe (10)   123
Fraser Hamilton (10)   124
Gabrielle Aitchison (10)   124

Amy Sullivan (10)	125
Nicholas Gallacher (11)	125
Courtney Craig (10)	126
Meghann Farrell (10)	126
Callum Creechan (10)	127
Alison Brophy (10)	127
Alison Tougher (10)	128
Dario Palazzo (10)	128
Clare Kerr (10)	129
Stephanie Robb (9)	129
Amanda McInally (10)	130
Kieran McGinnes (10)	130
Sarah Aitchison (9)	130
Megan Finnigan (10)	131
Christopher Murray (10)	131
Alissa McGuigan (9)	131

St Mary's Primary School, Lanark

Connor McEwan (9)	132
Stephen Hilland (9)	132
Rebecca Scott (10)	133
Danielle Stewart (10)	134
Sarah McQuoney (9)	134
Callum Johnstone (10)	135
Christopher Cunningham (10)	135
Ainsley Stark (11)	136
Kenneth Craig (10)	136
Roseanna Johnstone (10)	137
Chloe Lamarra (11)	137
Esmée Gallagher (10)	138
Gregor Frame (10)	138
Helena Davidson (10)	139
Scott Ellis (11)	139
Nicole Sykes (10)	140
Craig Bustard (10)	140
Erin McLeod (10)	141
Jamie Cooper (8)	141
Lesley Simpson (10)	142

Sacred Heart Primary School

Emma Shields (10)	142
Shannon Gordon (10)	143
Alex Craig (10)	143
Gemma Nicol (10)	144
Chelsea Porter (10)	144
Melissa Dougan (10)	145
Gary McAlpine (10)	145
Abbie Sloan (10)	146

Woodhead Primary School

Hannah Victoria Black (10)	147
Andrew McDougall (10)	147
Jordan Roy (11)	148
Kimberley Fleming (11)	148
Taylor Jeffrey (10)	149
Kirsty Craig (10)	149
Stuart Macdonald (10)	150
Scott Jannaway (10)	150
Cameron Humphreys (10)	151
Jennifer Gray (10)	151
Allison Day (10)	152
Fraser McEwan (10)	152
Laura Garvin (10)	153
Hazel Connolly (10)	153
Mary-Jo Getliffe (10)	154

The Poems

Seasons

In the spring flowers start to grow,
In the winter it begins to snow.
In the summer the sun is shining,
In the autumn the leaves are golden.

In the summer my sister likes to play,
But in the winter she cries all day.
Her tears are like the autumn showers,
But her smile is nicer than the summer flowers.

In the summer I went out to sea
And my granny was watching, drinking her tea.
First it's spring, then it's summer,
Then autumn and winter run into one another.

In the winter Santa is calling,
While the white snow keeps on falling.
Santa might get very upset
If you don't look after your new pet.

Oriana D'Aguanno (9)
Alexandra Primary School

Football

F ootball is really cool,
O utdoors all the time
O n the ball is Richard Kane
T rying new ball tricks
B etter than yesterday
A lways trying to be better
L ove football
L ove life.

A didas
N ike
D iadora.

M y
E verlasting dream is to be a football superstar!

Richard Kane (9)
Alexandra Primary School

My Dogs

My name is Colette,
I have a pet.
We play
Especially on a sunny day.
His name is Barney,
I call him Arnie.
We play games
And rhyme names.
My dad bought another
To annoy my mother.
His name is Buster,
I call him Duster.
My dad calls him Pup,
I am always lifting him up.
Please don't let him buy another
To annoy my mother.
'A Russian terrier,' he said,
If he does he'll be dead,
Help!

Colette Connelly (9)
Alexandra Primary School

The Only Girl

I live in a boy's world
Full of games and footballs,
No dolls or ribbons apparent in our house.
If only I had a sister it would be so much fun,
We could share a pink bedroom
And fill it with dolls,
Go to the shops instead of the match,
I'd have a lifelong friend
Who would bring so much joy,
But I am the only girl in a boy's world!

Sian Fitzpatrick (9)
Alexandra Primary School

The Seaside

I enjoy a paddle in the sea,
The water comes up over my knees,
It's wide and clear for me to see,
All the living creatures in the sea.

On sunny days,
We go to the beach,
The water is always within reach,
We like to go in the sea
And have a go on a fast jet-ski.

The sea can be so much fun,
Especially in the midday sun,
You can jump about, splash and play
And have a really great day.

I build a sandcastle in the sand,
Then I smack it down with my hand,
The sea comes in and washes it away,
Need to build one another day.

Sara Mulvaney (9)
Alexandra Primary School

My Cat

I got my cat when I was eight
And I wondered why I felt so great.
My cat was golden in colour.

It went out the window for a stroll
And every day it comes back
And decides to stay.

I go to bed at nine o'clock,
My cat comes in at 12 o'clock
And snuggles up next to me,
Hunting's over for the day,
Sleep is now its destiny.

My cat's name is Jacks.

Paul Breen (9)
Alexandra Primary School

My Best Football Team

Celtic is my favourite team,
Every time they score I let out a scream.
Chris Sutton on the ball,
Every time he skins them all.
Celtic versus Rangers, here we go,
Come on the Hoops
Give us a show.
We, the fans, stand in the crowd
Singing, 'Hail, hail', we feel proud.
Here we go, the end is near,
The Celtic fans have nothing to fear.
We have done it again,
We have won,
We have beaten our old friends 2-1.

Dale Andrew (9)
Alexandra Primary School

The Ocean

The ocean you see
Is an ocean so blue!
It lights up the sky so bright and new!
The fish that swim there
Are so happy and free,
Just the way I like to be.

The octopus you see
Is an octopus so free
And swims with glee!
And that's the way I want it to be.

There is a special fish
Which goes swish, swish, swish.
I nearly forgot
The nasty shark
That has a terrible attack.

Alicia Zambonini (10)
Alexandra Primary School

I Wish . . .

I wish, I wish I had a dog,
It would be my best friend.
I would take it everywhere,
Even round the bend.

I wish I was a pop star
And I was able to sing.
I would go round the country
With my bling-bling-bling.

I wish I could go on a shopping spree
With my true best friend,
I would shop all day
And spend, spend, spend.

A wish is very special,
It can make you feel okay,
But if you wish too much
You could wish your life away.

Emma Merry (10)
Alexandra Primary School

Our Great Playground

In our playground we have fun,
Especially in the sun,
We run around and around,
Until we fall on the ground.

All the boys play ball,
Then you hear them call,
When the ball goes in the net,
All the boys are glad they met.

We love our playground,
It is great,
We have fun with our mates
Inside our school gates.

Stacey Carswell (9)
Alexandra Primary School

A Puppy-Dog's Tale

With two Lhasa apsos our house was quite busy,
Then along comes a third and Mum's in a tizzy,
With grooming and bathing, preparing for a show,
The dogs are now ready and waiting to go.

I stood at the ringside and my heart pounded,
My dog got 1st prize and I was astounded.
With a trophy in my hand and a smile on my face,
The judge said my dog was so full of grace.

So, it's off now to Crufts the world's biggest show,
It's held down in Birmingham, a long way to go,
With shampoos, brushes, lotions and potions.
Please let him behave, not make a commotion.
So on the 11th of March tune in your TV,
You never know, you might even see *me!*

Ryan Hanlon (9)
Alexandra Primary School

Dancing Queen

Dancing light and airy,
But there is no way
I am a dancing fairy.
I point my toes,
I spin around
And I touch the ground.

The rhythm, the beat,
Everyone we meet
Is tapping their feet.

The music is good,
It puts us in a mood.
Our dancing is not a test,
But we try to do our best.
My dancing, your dancing,
Everyone's dancing.

Lauren McDade (10)
Alexandra Primary School

One Hallowe'en Night

One Hallowe'en night
When the moon shone bright,
All the ghosts and ghouls came out for the night
And the famous Count Dracula was looking for someone to bite.

One Hallowe'en night
When the moon shone bright,
There was a vampire bat
Who spooked a young cat,
The cat ran onto the road and it went *splat!*

One Hallowe'en night
When the moon shone bright,
There was a wicked witch, a wicked old witch,
She had a twin, you couldn't tell which witch was which.
They fell off their brooms into a deep, dark ditch,
No one saw the witch twins ever again,
After they fell into that deep, dark ditch.
Boo!

Kathryn McGoldrick (10)
Alexandra Primary School

My Football Team

Football, football is my dream,
Celtic, Celtic is my team!
I would love to run onto a football park,
When all the fans give out a hark.
I have the ball, I score a goal!
I give out a big yippee!
Now all the fans really like me,
Celtic, Celtic is my team,
That's why football is my dream.
Champions Leagues and World Cups,
Dillon Finesy picks up the cup.

Dillon Finesy (10)
Alexandra Primary School

Fright Night

I was lying in my bed
having a bad dream.
I was walking towards a house
and then I screamed!
Ten blood-sucking zombies
standing in a row.
They wanted my bones
to throw.

Andrew Whitelaw (8)
Braidwood Primary School

Happy

My best feeling is happy
Happy, joyful, happy
Happy is friendly
Happy is playful
Happy is a feeling
I was happy when I went to the park
Happy, joyful, happy.

Gemma McDonald (8)
Braidwood Primary School

I Feel Scared

I got a fright
in the middle of the night.
I saw a robber in the house
being as quiet as a mouse.
The alarm went off.
He took off.

Ross Elder (8)
Braidwood Primary School

Recycling

R ubbish you put in your bin.
E nvironment we must keep clean.
C arelessly people throw rubbish away.
Y ou have to make the effort
C hildren must all try to do better.
L and is messy with litter.
I magine how nice it would be if everyone tried their best.
N ever drop litter ever again.
G o and put rubbish in the proper bin.

Samantha Bunch (11)
Carluke Primary School

Friends

F reedom from school, here comes Saturday
R ough rugby, we play, hooray!
I nvitations to party
E nd of the day and we are still out to play
N ever calm, never still, all this way until . . .
D ashing through the woods all day
S kateboarding in the skate park all day.

Peter Allen (11)
Carluke Primary School

Friends

F riends are good to ten-year-olds
R ainbows show when we're on the go
I t's impossible to see us
E xciting to have friends with you
N ever fall out with your friends
D avid is one of my friends who lives in Liverpool
S ings silly songs to me.

Martin Reid (11)
Carluke Primary School

Football

F ootball is the game.
O ut on the pitch I like to be.
O n the TV, I like to watch football.
T he ball got saved on the line.
B ut there were plenty more to come.
A ll the fans were singing and cheering.
L oud as they could be.
L oving their team to win.

Ryan Gilmour (11)
Carluke Primary School

The Accident

The car goes fast,
A bus drives past,
Children play,
On a bright sunny day.

A ball rolls to the street,
One boy's quick on his feet,
He runs straight out,
Thinking no traffic's about.

But . . . too late,
He cannot escape,
A screech of brakes,
The bus and car makes.

Trembling he lies,
Shaken by surprise,
The drivers are in shock,
Lots of people flock.

He should have stopped,
Looked and listened, but did not,
Road safety's the key,
For everyone, including me.

Christopher McIntyre (11)
Cathedral Primary School

Un Arc-en-ciel

There are lots of colours in the rainbow
like blue and yellow and pink,
there are also lots of coloured pens
with different coloured ink.
My favourite colours are pink and gold
which sparkles in the sun,
I also think they go with games
which are so very fun.
Red and crimson are the colours
when lovers have just met,
they sit on a bench looking at the waves
until the sun has set.
I know all the colours of the rainbow
are very beautiful to see,
but don't go following the pot of gold
for it is left for me.

Kirsty Findlay (11)
Cathedral Primary School

In The Park

Down in the park
I met a girl called Sally
Who said, 'Go away,
I am trying to practice my ballet.'

I walked along to the pond
I did not want to go beyond
I sat on the bench and fed a duck
I look at my shoes, they are covered in muck.

I sat on the swing
And heard an old lady sing
Her voice was so loud
It attracted a crowd.

David Dunsmore (11)
Cathedral Primary School

My Gran

My gran is on a diet
She said, 'You ought to try it.'
No more treats for you
No more sweets or Irn Bru.
For breakfast it's all nuts 'n bran.
I said, 'I cannot eat that Gran!'
For lunch it's bread and honey,
I thought that Granny was acting funny.
Tea was not much better,
So I wrote her a personal letter . . .
Nuts for breakfast,
For me won't do,
So now I'm going home,
To get my Irn Bru.

Stephen Garrity (11)
Cathedral Primary School

Minnie And Winnie

Minnie and Winnie
Slept in a shell
Sleep little ladies
And they slept very well.
Pink was the shell
With thin silver throughout,
Sounds of the great sea
Wandered about.
Sleep little ladies
Wake not too soon,
Sleep very deeply
In the light of the moon.

Nicholas Divers (11)
Cathedral Primary School

The Simpsons

Simpsons, they're the Simpsons, they are amusing and funny
They live in Springfield where it is usually sunny.
They are no ordinary family
They have yellow skin and four fingers.
Lisa she is very smart
She watches Itchy and Scratchy with her brother Bart.
Then there is Homer, he's absolutely lazy,
When Bart annoys him he goes crazy.
Marge is wise
There is hardly anything she doesn't despise.
Maggie, she loves her mummy
But even more she loves her dummy.
Bart he is so bad
And he doesn't always get on with his dad.
Last of all there is Grandpa Abraham Simpson,
His stories are boring,
When they are told everyone is snoring.

Max Robinson (11)
Cathedral Primary School

My Dream Of A Kitten

I would like a little kitten,
But once my mum was bitten,
She is allergic to their hair,
I think it's so unfair!
So we had to settle for a fish,
Oh my God how I wish,
For a cat or a pretty puppy
And *not* a little guppy!

Naomi O'Rourke (11)
Cathedral Primary School

My Dog Jake

I have a dog, his name is Jake,
He likes a walk down by the lake
And when it comes to supper time,
He beats me home every time,
I like to brush his long, shiny coat,
To do away with all the knots.

Jake is a chihuahua, small and short,
Who loves to go for very long walks,
And when we walk along the riverbank,
He gets up to all sorts of pranks.
Jake is friendly, Jake is wise,
He also has big, loveable eyes.

At the end of the day I have to say,
We both are out of energy.

Shaun Nailen (11)
Cathedral Primary School

Shipwreck

One minute they were on the deck
The next, they were involved in a disastrous shipwreck.

Captain Smith and his men
Swam towards their hidden den.

As the Germans hunted for their prey
The Royal Navy waited for them at Liverpool bay.

When the Germans were at their full strength
It seemed they could rip through any defence.

But Captain Smith and the other survivors
Took turns to go down as deep-sea divers.

They got some food from the boat
And then they brought it back afloat.

Christopher Murray (11)
Cathedral Primary School

On Holiday

I love going on holiday, especially to Greece or Spain
And luckily we have never had a single spot of rain.
I like to relax in the sun or maybe play in the sand,
One time it was so hot I nearly burnt my hand.
I love their food, it is really good, especially their hot kebabs.
I love going in the swimming pool and giving my dad a race,
He finds it really hard to keep up with my fast pace.
I like to get a cold drink and play some volleyball,
Which I find quite difficult because I am not very tall.
This year I am going to Greece, I hope it will be warm
And I hope we don't ever get a storm.

Paul Davis (11)
Cathedral Primary School

If Only

If only I won the lottery,
A million pounds would do,
I would spend the money quickly
And enjoy it while I do.

I'd spend it on my family
And take them to Corfu,
But after this I would spend the money
On you know who.

I would buy some sparkling jewellery,
Only gold would do,
I would buy a fancy sports car
In either red or blue.

Designer clothes, I'd pierce my nose
Then probably queue up for the 'brew'
'Cause in the end, I'd be skint like you!

Oh, if only . . .

Caragh O'Brien (11)
Cathedral Primary School

Family

Family is the greatest gift
That you will ever have,
You join together with them
To chat and cry and laugh.

Sometimes they are really nice
And make you feel so good,
But sometimes they get on your nerves
And get you in a mood.

Family is always there
No matter what you do,
Even if you don't get on
You love them a lot - don't you?

Mums, when they are angry,
Can really drive you mad,
But they can also be very caring
This makes you feel so glad.

Dads on the other hand
Can really be quite fun,
Except when they're embarrassing
This makes you want to run.

When it comes to sisters and brothers
There's not much to say,
Except that they're annoying
But still good to have a play.

So all in all
Families are great
No matter what
They'll always remain your true mates.

Paula Jane Graham (11)
Cathedral Primary School

Going On Holiday

Waiting in the airport
To go on holiday
I've been excited forever
Probably since May.
In just one hour
I'll be on a plane
And I'll be hoping
That it won't rain.
We're going to departures
To sit and wait
And I'll be wondering
If I'll meet a mate.
The weather will be sunny
And hopefully bright,
But it will be dark
During the night.
We're going on the plane
To take our seat
And I'll be roasted
By the heat.
It's a long and weary journey
But soon we'll be there
Out in the sunshine
And in the fresh air.
Tenerife here we come
For two weeks in the sun
We'll play in the pool
And we're bound to have fun.

Lisa Rattigan (11)
Cathedral Primary School

My Friends

My friend's name is Jennifer
She's really, really nice
But she's always up for a challenge
An indoor girl is she!

Clare-Louise is a real good friend
Always up for a laugh
She's always there when I need her
Like Jennifer she's a real good friend!

Another friend of mine is Natasha
I really, really like her
When I've got a problem
She is always there!

Amanda is a funny friend
She always makes me laugh
We go to Guides every Monday night
And having fun with her isn't really hard!

So these are all my very best friends!
They're always fun to be with!
They're such a good laugh
And they're the best friends I could ever have!

Shannen Black (11)
Cathedral Primary School

Beat Bullying

B ullying is terrible and horrible to experience
U nderstanding a bully's mind is impossible
L aughing and joking, covering up your feelings
L aughing and joking whilst only you are suffering
Y ou are scared so you don't tell anyone
I nterval and breaks usually good but now a dread
N ow you finally see sense and tell someone
G oing to school is happy and fun.

Michael Devlin (11)
Cathedral Primary School

My Goldfish

My goldfish is called Toast,
He is golden, tiny and I love him the most,
His sharp little tail, whooshes about all day,
When I go near the tank, he always wants to play.

He has small round eyes,
That look like delicious apple pies,
The gills on his side, go in and out
And he has a little red spot on the top of his snout.

Toast hunts down and gobbles his food up,
Before you can say, 'Tut, tut, tut.'
My little goldfish hides behind a plant,
When he hears about a tiny little ant.

You can never catch a glimpse of him,
Because he's so fast with his tiny little fin,
He's definitely a sly wee Toast,
But my precious fish, I still love him the most.

Heather McDonald (11)
Cathedral Primary School

Winter Wonders

Winter is coming, falling fluttering snow,
I can tell by the weather, everyone should know,
If you go out the door you'll see that I'm right,
Piles of snow even whiter than white.

Winter is games, snowball fights,
Snowmen, snow angels, in early at night,
Chattering teeth heard through the air,
Snow sticking in children's hair.

Winter is danger, accidents on roads,
Drivers not following the Highway Code,
Old people falling with broken bones,
No more heating for your cosy homes.

Andrew Guthrie (11)
Cathedral Primary School

Hallowe'en

H allowe'en's theme, terror and fright
A ll ghouls and spirits come out that night
L ong, children stand eager for their sweets
L oudly parents groan as their children munch their treats
O ut come the witches, vampires and ghosts
W anting all the sweets, eating some, well perhaps most
E ach child says nearly exactly the same
E ach joke, each act, I wish they never came
N ext, when Hallowe'en comes round to you, I'd watch my back
  if I were you!

Julia Perrie (11)
Cathedral Primary School

My Pet Hamster

Charlie Murphy is my pet hamster
He is always such a prankster
He runs up and down his helter-skelter
Charlie Murphy is a belter
He eats lots of different food, he even likes pasta
Charlie knows there is no hamster faster.

Jordan Murphy (11)
Cathedral Primary School

Spiders

Spiders are black, spiders are hairy
Some people say they are very scary
They are big and small, but worst of all
Is when they can't see them at all
They frighten you, bite you and crawl up your legs
Speaking of spiders, there's one on your head!

Andrew Shields (11)
Cathedral Primary School

Flowers

F rom daisies to snowdrops not one looks the same
L ong ones and short ones, bright ones and dark ones
O ur gardens are full of them
W hen summertime comes
E ach one is unique, not one is the same
R oses and tulips dance in the night
S unflowers stand tall and bright.

Dominique Larkin (11)
Cathedral Primary School

Puppies

I love puppies, they are small and cute
I love it when they eat my socks
I think it's funny when they do tricks
I think it's cool the way they fetch sticks
I love the ones that are small and fluffy
I also like the ones that are fat and puffy.

Steven Hart (11)
Cathedral Primary School

Granny

G reat grannies always are
R ight, but never wrong and they are
A lways late for a date.
N ice grannies say they are not
N aughty and always say they are
Y oung and not old.

Connor Gallen (11)
Cathedral Primary School

My Family

My family are kind and caring, anyone can see
There is my mum and dad, and of course there is me
My mum is tall and very thin
She is so thin, as thin as a pin
My dad likes football and he is lots of fun
He is my hero, he is my number one
I am Mum and Dad's favourite, their only son.

I love my family, I really do
If you met them you would too
We like to go to KFC
That is my mum, dad and don't forget me.

Even though my family is so very small
We are part of God's family, one and all
I love my family, I really do
And pray to God you love yours too.

Kieran Moore (11)
Cathedral Primary School

Mum

In the morning when you look like a bear,
Your mum's the one who'll fix your hair.
Even if you find a tug,
She'll be there to give you a hug.

When you hurt yourself,
She'll give you a plaster and say,
'It's not a disaster.'

When she complains that she's fat,
You think she's a grumpy old bat.

When you're feeling sad,
She'll say it's not that bad,
So I am always glad that my mum is there.

Rosheen Patel (11)
Cathedral Primary School

My Best Friend

My best friend is caring and fun
My best friend could talk to anyone
She is a great friend
I know she wouldn't pretend.

My best buddy has long black hair
And she really, really, really does care
My best friend has very pale skin
And she is also nice and thin.

My best friend has three goldfish
And her favourite card game is go fish
Her favourite colour is pink
And Coca-Cola she likes to drink.

My best friend's name is Amanda Miller
I think my friend is the best in the world.

Clare Louise Boyle (11)
Cathedral Primary School

From My Heart Just For You Gran

You have a heart of gold
Even though you're very old
I want to say thank you
For everything you do.
It's so cheerful to see your smiling face
So don't ever let it slip away.
I love you, I love you,
I do, I do!
So for the last time
Thank you!

Emma McNulty (11)
Cathedral Primary School

My Granny

Do you know my granny?
She's really old and wrinkly.
She sits all day
With nothing to do
Except watch the TV.

Have you met my granny?
She's always full of fun.
She gives me sweets and chocolate
When I'm feeling glum.

I've always loved my granny,
She loves me like my mum.
When I'm feeling sad and lonely,
She makes me feel *number one.*

So now you know my granny,
It's pretty obvious to see
That I love her
And she loves me.

Christopher Costello (11)
Cathedral Primary School

Winter

A dark, gloomy season,
Snowy hilltops rule the landscape.

A clean, fresh season,
Snow falls gently like bubbles floating in the air.

A blanket of fluff melts to create water,
A warm bath is always welcomed after a muddy park.

Hot chocolate and toast for supper sitting by the fire,
And tucked up in bed all safe and warm as dusk falls.

John Robertson (11)
Cathedral Primary School

Dreams

Dreams are hopes of fantasies which come true,
Where the skies are green and the grass is blue.

Dreams are peaceful but some are not, some people call it frightmare!
But others call it . . . a nightmare.

Dreams fulfil our heart's desires,
With gold and ruby sapphires.

Dreams which have comfy beds,
Or funny clowns with big heads.

Dreams are the land of nod,
Where I met a guy called Todd.

But when it comes to the end,
Goodbye my dreamland friend.

Natasha Gaittens (11)
Cathedral Primary School

My Best Friend

My best friend has lovely, long, auburn hair
My best friend has glistening green eyes
My best friend has smooth tanned skin
My best friend has beautiful long legs.

My best friend is loving and caring
My best friend is kind and considerate
My best friend cheers you up when you're sad
My best friend helps you through hard times.

My best friend is the best in the world
My best friend's name is Clare Louise Boyle.

Amanda Miller (11)
Cathedral Primary School

Dolphins

Dolphins are good, dolphins are fine,
I really wish one was mine.
They splash in the sea and jump with glee,
I really love them,
They really love me.

Dolphins are wonderful,
Dolphins are swell,
To swim with them is brilliant,
I personally can tell.
To swim with dolphins is a delight,
I wish I could swim with them every night.

Dolphins are fast,
When out in the ocean you might see some swim past.
If dolphins could talk to us I am sure they would say,
'Come on into the water and we will play all day.'

Dolphins are swift and so carefree,
If you meet a dolphin, I am sure you'll agree.

Andrew Mitchell (11)
Cathedral Primary School

It's A Dog's Life

My dog Bouncer is as lazy as my mum,
He lies in bed all day with his legs stretched out,
He hates doing exercise, he loves chasing cats,
He always lies on his dirty doggie mat,
    But that's just Bouncer.

He runs about the house with the burst ball in his mouth,
He's crazy, but fun,
To me he's number 1
I love him so much
    But that's just Bouncer.

Carly Louise Gardner (11)
Cathedral Primary School

Magical Creatures

Pixies are perfect but annoying I might add.
Dragons are dangerous and protective you might say.
Elves are exciting creatures and helpful to all.
Trolls are treacherous creatures but extremely stupid you will say.
Leprechauns are lucky Irish folk and hide their pots of gold.
Gnomes are great, happy creatures all day,
But they are sad and gloomy creatures at night.
Mermaids are marvellous and happy creatures.
Unicorns are united creatures and are really playful.
I could go on forever naming these creatures
Like dwarfs or fairies but I think I'll stop there,
And I hope you enjoyed it.

Jennifer Mullaney (11)
Cathedral Primary School

Scotland

Scotland, my gracious home,
cold and chilly and very frilly.
In the summer it's not too warm
and not too cold.

Scotland, my gracious home,
filled with glory and achievement.
Its people are proud and brave
with what its nation's done.

Scotland, my gracious home,
filled with joy and laughter.
It makes you feel as if you are flying,
for I am proud of my nation and home.
Scotland.

Gavin Hall (10)
Cathedral Primary School

Rock Star

I want to be a rock star
Be able to play and sing
Strum the guitar and write cool tunes
And wait for the agents to ring

The crowds will adore me
They'll scream and they'll shout
'Look everybody
There's a rock star about.'

My band will be with me
To help me along
Friendship and laughter
And of course lots of songs.

I'll make lots of money
Travel places afar
In my flash silver limo
A real superstar.

Stephen Archibald (11)
Cathedral Primary School

The War

Hitler started the war.
People of Britain had to prepare.
Bomb shelters, blackouts,
Gas masks to protect them
from fighter planes in the air.

Children, adults, soldiers,
everyone around.
They were frightened, tired
and miserable under the ground.

Oliver Reilly (11)
Cathedral Primary School

Football

Football is my favourite sport,
I play it twice a week,
I bought brand new football boots,
My very own to keep.

The sport can be quite tiring,
It keeps me on my toes,
It can get quite competitive,
But never comes to blows.

I really have got very good,
I would score every game if I could,
Teams I often cream,
I suppose that explains why I'm now in the dream team.

Ryan McCluskey (11)
Cathedral Primary School

A Dog Is For Life

A dog is for life,
you should never forget.
From puppy to old age, it may need a vet.
It's there to be walked,
to be fed and brushed,
but most of all it will need to be loved.
It has the same feelings as you and me,
It wants to run, play and be free.
So a dog is for life
and never forget,
it's there to be loved,
cherished and kept.

Daniel Cerretti (10)
Cathedral Primary School

Theme Parks

In the park there are many rides,
Dodgems, teacups and lots of slides.
Stampedia is the fastest train ride in the park,
Temple Del Fuego gets full marks.

Shows are staged throughout the day,
Each country a place to laugh and play.
Simulator rides are very rare,
Ocean Odyssey is the best one there.

Relax on the boats, admire the view,
Travel the rails along with the crew.
Dance the cancan if you dare,
On a visit to the Wild West take care.

The water parks are really cool,
To miss it you would be a fool.
Fight the rapids, jump the waves
Slide the flumes, as dark as caves.

Port Aventura is my favourite place,
Tropical sunshine and lots of space.
A holiday to remember, good fun for all,
If you go in the summer or even in the fall.

Matthew MacDermid (11)
Cathedral Primary School

May Your Heart Be

May your heart be happy,
May your heart be bright.

May your roads be smooth,
And your burdens light.

May you find your dreams,
May you touch your star.

May you never forget
Just how special you are.

Amy Halloran (11)
Cathedral Primary School

Tsunami

What can you hear?
Water splashing, waves ascending,
Crescendo,
Rear up, come back down,
People screaming, mumbling prayers.

What can you feel?
Icy cold water lashing against my body,
Drenched,
Horrified, traumatised,
Annoyed with God.

What can you see?
Babies crying, people running,
Even the most courageous,
Water banging on all grounds,
People shouting to take to your heels.

What do you do?
Gather your family,
Gather your friends,
Get into a room,
Get on high grounds.

What do you hope for?
Hope for it to be OK,
Hope for it to go away,
Sing a song, say a prayer,
Come out when it's all over.

Robyn Docherty (10)
Coalburn Primary School

Tsunami

What can you hear?
Sudden crash of waves coming,
Creaking, shuddering, gasping,
Roaring wind whistling,
Help!

What can you feel?
It is warm but I feel cold,
My body is wobbling,
I am nervous,
What should I do?

What can you see?
All I see is people vanishing,
Waves are rising,
Destroying homes,
Devastation!

What do you do?
Run to save as many people as I can,
Shout, run, scream, pray,
Try not to panic,
Protect the people I love.

Lauren Blair (9)
Coalburn Primary School

Apples

An apple is like a golden desert when the sun shines on it.
Apples are crunchy like hard stones.
The seeds in an apple are like little rabbit droppings.

An apple skin is like the peelings of a carrot or potato.
The inside of an apple is like the colour of a custard cream.

Rory Hillan (9)
Coalburn Primary School

Pasta

My pasta is like bows in a girl's hair
It is sometimes very curly like ribbon
Pasta comes in different shapes
But I like bows best.

Pasta is usually orange or yellow like a sunset
When it's orange it's cheesy
Pasta is so tasty like sweets
When it's yellow and covered with butter
It is like a melting ice lolly.

Pasta is as long as a limousine
But as small as a crumb
It can be al dente like chewing gum
Pasta can also be overcooked and soggy like Weetabix.

Heather Ross (10)
Coalburn Primary School

Lollies

A lolly is like a marble on a twig,
It can be the colours of the rainbow.
A lolly is sweet just like honey,
It can also be as sour as a lemon.

A lolly is like a stone because it does not break,
It is as hard as a skull.
When a lolly is thrown it hurts,
A rock is stronger though.
When you bite it, it threatens to break your teeth.

A lolly can be a cube or cylinder shape,
It looks like it wears a wedding ring.
Lollies are as good as a day off school,
They taste like honey and lemon.

Guy Bernard (10)
Coalburn Primary School

Earthquakes

What can you hear?
Loud fragments of shattering and screaming,
Rumbling noises,
Right under your feet,
Help!

What can you feel?
Vibrations of rocks,
The ground breaking underneath my feet,
My heart is pounding like someone hitting drums,
Run!

What can you see?
All you can see is people disappearing,
Low rumbling noises are rising,
Destroying people's houses,
Devastation!

Tamsin Stewart (9)
Coalburn Primary School

Dinosaurs

D inosaurs are very big
I n the jungle you hear a rumble and a tumble
N ever get in their way
O r otherwise they'll stamp you away
S tegosaurus is so spiky with pointed nails and spiky tail
A tiny dinosaur might look cute but when you go near
   it snaps, snaps, snaps
U nder the sea never go diving
R un away from T-rex you'll never stand a chance
   because he is always there
S o never get in their way or you'll be squashed away.

Jordan Jarvie (8)
Kirkshaws Primary School

Dinosaurs

D inosaurs are so big
I f they were with us
N othing would be left
O h the gentlest dinosaur would be diplodocus
S tegosaurus would be the strongest
A nd T-rex would be the fiercest
U nder water there would be dinosaurs too
R ough and strong
S o dinosaurs might eat you.

Sean Gibson (8)
Kirkshaws Primary School

Winter

W inter, winter is so cold
I n winter I get up at night and dress by yellow candlelight
N ice, nice, the snow is nice
T he ice is so, so slippery
E veryone is having fun
R un, run in the winter sun.

Nicole Anderson (8)
Kirkshaws Primary School

Dinosaurs

Dinosaurs, dinosaurs, I love dinosaurs
Dinosaurs big, dinosaurs small
I love dinosaurs no matter how long
Dinosaurs spiky, dinosaurs stripy
If I had a dinosaur I would call it Mikey
Dinosaurs, dinosaurs, I love dinosaurs.

Ryan Lucas (8)
Kirkshaws Primary School

School

School, school is the best
Teachers test children
My teacher is the best
My teacher is cool
She lets us paint
It's fun, fun, fun
School, school is the best.

Holly Drummond (8)
Kirkshaws Primary School

World

W orld, world so big and wide
O ceans and countryside
R ound, round, day and night
L ight, light all the time
D eep, deep, fishes swim in the ocean deep.

World, world we love you.

Claire Marshall (8)
Kirkshaws Primary School

Holidays

I like to go on holiday,
We go in a plane to get there.
At the hotel I play in the pool,
Because the sun is hot and it keeps me cool.
I make new friends,
But say bye-bye when my holiday ends.

Aaron Rae (8)
Kirkshaws Primary School

School

S chool, school, school is super cool
C ome and join the fun
H ow is school so, so cool?
O ur teacher uses good stickers for good work
O pen up your books and do good work
L ots of children are having fun in the sun.

Thomas Young (9)
Kirkshaws Primary School

Winter Where Are You?

Winter, winter where are you?
Winter, winter what do you do?
Winter, winter how do you feel?
Winter where are you?
Winter how do you feel?

Hannah Grennen (7)
Kirkshaws Primary School

Colours

Red is the colour of the carpet stairs I walk down.
Blue is the colour of the deep blue sea.
Green is the colour of the grass where footballers play.
Orange is the colour of the juicy orange.
Black is the colour of the dark at night.
White is the colour of the snow falling onto Earth.
Pink is the colour of a girl's birthday.
Yellow is the colour of the sand between your toes.
Silver is the colour of a diamond ring on your finger.
Gold is the colour of a star in the night sky.

Chloe Craig (11)
Knowetop Primary School

The Butterfly

A lovely little butterfly came flying past me,
not an ordinary butterfly, more extraordinary than a bee.

Its wings were yellow with big blue spots,
well they weren't that big, not much bigger than dots.

Its body was black with green squiggles,
and when it moves they start to wriggle.

What will I name it? I thought and thought,
maybe I will name it Starky, like a robot.

I would name it Silky, if it had a fur coat,
or I would call it Beardy, if it were a goat.

If it were a horse, I would call it Midge,
if it were a jellyfish it would be called Squidge.

I cannot think of a name,
what shall I call it?

I will name it 'Surprise',
'cause there are too many wonderful names.

Marissa Clarke (11)
Knowetop Primary School

Autumn

The wind was blowing,
The trees were swaying,
The leaves were falling,
Then autumn came.

Wrap up warm,
Hats and scarves,
Gloves and mittens,
Even wrap up your kittens.

Look around and you will find
Everything is turning brown.

Melissa Dickie (11)
Knowetop Primary School

Friends

I sat on a chair and looked at the sky
and watched the cars that went zooming by.

My friend came round to comfort me
and ended up staying for tea.

We decided to go out and play
and I really had a fantastic day.

She came round the next day
we bought some sweets and I did pay.

On the way home we met our pals
and they truly are the bestest gals.

There's Yvonne, Charlie, Becca, Melissa
Wallis, Hannah, Lynsey, Marissa.

They're the best girls I've ever met
and they're the best friends I could ever get.

Laura Scott (11)
Knowetop Primary School

All The Colours Of The Rainbow

Red you should have stayed in bed
because it is warm and cosy.

Black is the colour of the midnight sky
if you go outside there is a black knight.

Blue is a nice colour
In the summer.

Yellow is the colour of the sun
and it is the colour that brightens up my day.

Pink is a nice light colour
and it is my friend's favourite colour.

Green is a colour
that can go into just about anything.

Iain Whyte (11)
Knowetop Primary School

Loopy People

Laura, she's the loopy one, always jumping about,
Sam, he's the silly one, everybody says he's a wee bairn.

Maira is the smart one,
She's always got her nose stuck in a book,
She's always at the top of the class.
Emma, she's the normal one, she's always jogging about.

Dean, he's awful fond of football,
Every time you see him he's always kicking a ball.
I'm all the same - I always jog, I always read
And all of that kind of stuff.
Well that's all of the loopy people for you.

Natalie Anderson (11)
Knowetop Primary School

Homework Oh Homework

Homework oh homework
Why are you there?
You haunt me all night
And give me nightmares!

I'd rather be watching
TV all day
'But homework is important!'
That's what the teacher would say!

You are there in my school bag
All weekend!
But if I don't do you
I'll have no pocket money to spend!

So I'll slave away
For hours and hours
Doing my homework
For our teacher, Miss Nowers.

Emma Craig (11)
Knowetop Primary School

The Orchestra

I went to Glasgow Concert Hall
To go and see the show
I bought myself a ticket
And sat down in the front row.

The orchestra man, the conductor
Came in and said, 'Hello'
But then he went to his stand
And finally said, 'Let's go!'

The violins started to fiddle quickly
While the double basses were playing very, very deeply
The harp was very high and the cello was very low
I would definitely come back to see this show.

The mighty tuba made a deafening sound
I was surprised the player was able to stay on the ground
The big trombone player was blowing very hard
But then I realised he was sitting on a tub of lard.

The show finished with a fanfare, then I went home
And heard a buzzing in my ear.

Scott Walker Gibson (11)
Knowetop Primary School

Wind

The wind like a vandal
Creeping round the corners
Whistling and howling
Just to scare you away

It lashes at doors
Just trying to get in
Looking for more trouble
As the trees sway in the breeze.

Everyone is rushing home
So they might be safe
As the umbrellas are breaking while it is raining
And the milk bottle derby just starts
As the wind gives them a boost.

The leaves rustle
As all the people stand on them
While the wind howls and pushes cars
From side to side.

It pushes as hard as it can
To break windows of houses
Ruining the town and leaving it a mess.

Scattered paper lies everywhere
As the people try to clean up the mess
But the vandal just gets to rest
As he lies sleeping in his bed.

Elliot Baker (11)
Knowetop Primary School

My Dad

My dad is super
he does things that people might not do,
he goes crazy in the car
and parks where you've not to.

He jumps up and down when Rangers score
and runs about the room,
he dances round the table
and falls with a boom.

When it comes to lunchtime
you wouldn't trust him with a spoon,
so all I get is a sandwich
and a drink of Irn Bru.

Let's not forget dinner,
it's the same thing all the time,
it just gets so boring
so what will I do?

It's time for bed
dreading the night ahead,
my dad snores so loudly
I get a sore head.

As it turns to morning
I face the day ahead
and will be getting ready
if Dad gets me out of bed.

Lauren Walker (11)
Knowetop Primary School

The Scary Monster

Something happened late last week,
I was climbing up the stairs to bed.
I heard a creak and my face went red,
I wondered what to do, who it was or where they went,
I think it was a monster.

When I reached my room and climbed into bed,
Two big hands were climbing in the window,
I ran out and shut the blind and curled up in bed and shut my eyes,
I'm sure it was a monster.

As I was getting up early in the morning,
My door swung open but no one was there.
I was scared standing in my night-time wear,
Yep, it was a monster.

When I was in the shower,
I heard a swooshing sound,
All around,
Definitely, positively a monster.

When I was changed I ran downstairs scared out of my wits,
I hid behind the sofa quiet as a mouse,
Then someone or something sat on the sofa,
'Argh!' I screamed and ran away,
Wanting to hide every day,
It *was* a monster.

When I was hid snuggled up in bed,
A few things came to my head,
I got up to look around,
But the monster had gone and was never coming back.

Hayley Caldwell (11)
Knowetop Primary School

On Dark Nights

Everybody's gone to bed
The lights have all gone off
I lie awake in my bed
Hearing *cough, cough, cough.*

Then I hear a howling wind
Whistling outside my house,
What does it want with me?
Why is it here? I've done nothing wrong.

There's pitter-patter on my roof
What can it be?
Is it a burglar visiting me?

Tap, tap, tap at my window,
Is it a monster trying to grab me?
And with its long, thin, bony fingers,
That look like claws, will it get me?

Then finally the morning comes
And everything's back to normal,
But what I don't know is
What lies ahead tonight!

Natalie Dunn (11)
Knowetop Primary School

School Is Borin'

School is borin', I feel like snorin'
Every day we do the same thing, maths (yawn), language (yawn)
Readin', 'Readin'! Are you kiddin' me?'
Why can't we come in at ten or eleven - not nine?
Surely it's a crime comin' in then, I'm still in ma bed at half eight.

OK, next subject, teachers always gettin' you into trouble
For the least wee thing
If you so much as squeak, they're doon yer neck,
Bawlin' their brains oot.
Just because they have big, comfy chairs and wooden desks
Doesn't mean they're bigger than you, it means they're . . . oh, forget it.
Teachers believe that in school all you need is work, work
And more work.

All us pupils think the same - the teachers are lame.
They give us homework on a Friday!
'What's that all about?' we shout.
How can we concentrate on a Saturday with homework on a Friday?
Three words - school is borin'!

Lynsey Harris (11)
Knowetop Primary School

A Borrower Who Became A King

There was an old lad
He looked very sad
He was weak and cold
Unlike my papa who was very bold

His life was just sorrow
All he did was borrow
He got whipped by the police
And got told to go east

Four years later a king came to town
He looked at the police with an angry frown
He stood up and took off his shirt
He had black marks on his back that looked like dirt

Oh my gosh, was this the poor lad
He looked very angry, nowhere near sad
His height was about 7 foot 9
His golden chariot had a glowing shine

Everyone recognised him and fell to their feet
All of the police force started to cry and weep
Oh king, give us a rest
Oh king, don't send us to death

OK, let it be
But don't make the same mistake with anybody else
That you made with me.

Usman Hussain (11)
Knowetop Primary School

The Dolphins

The dolphins leap in and out of the water
Making waves behind them
Like little children playing with their friends
Swimming below where the fishes play
Swimming deeper than the sharks' prey
Then they come back up to the top
To play jump over the waves, they find this fun
When it is time to go away
Leaping towards the sun at sunset
In the morning they come out again
And chase alongside the great ship
Saying hello to all people abroad
They see people jump off the ship
To come and swim with them
They squeal and jump and laugh about
Until the people climb back on-board
Then they find another to chase
But when there are no more to chase
They go and find some friends
Jumping once more over the waves again and again
And that is the life of a dolphin.

Megan Hannah (11)
Knowetop Primary School

Paper

So much paper,
I don't know what to do.
From sugar paper to blue
And that's just a few!

There's so much paper
And only certain space
There's graph paper
And coloured too!

Paper can be used
In many, many ways
From paper aeroplanes to story writing
Oh thank God we have paper.

Paint to pencil, paper can hold most things,
Even markers but beware
If used to much it's sure to crack
Paper comes in black and white,
Yellow and red and many more colours.

Laura McGlashan (11)
Knowetop Primary School

Old Maw And Paw

Ma maw is startin' tae git some grey hair
an' ma paw is tae.
Ma paw says it's 'cause o' ma big sis an' me
gein him stress but it isnae.
They jist will nae admit they're gitting old.

Then one nicht we wir aw sitten' doon talkin'
An' then oor maw an' paw just blurted oot,
'It's 'cause we're gitten old!'

Debbie Kelly (11)
Knowetop Primary School

The Great Green Grub

'Yuck! Mum what's this?'
'It's my very own special dish.'
'But Mum, what is the green stuff?'
'They're vegetables, they make you tough.'
'I don't know if I want this Mummy.'
'You'll eat it or you'll have an empty tummy.'
'But Mum, it doesn't look nice.'
'Be quiet or you'll be onto rice!'
'Mum, where's the chips?'
'None of them, they go straight to your hips.'
'Mum, I don't want it, so can I watch TV?'
'No you cannot, you'll stay here with me!'
'I don't really want it. *Please Mum!*'
'Go on! You haven't even tried some.'
'OK, I'll have a wee nibble.'
'That's it, now watch you don't dribble!'
'Hmm, Mum this is OK!'
'See, I told you! I think we'll have this every day.'
'Oh Mum!'

Róisín King (11)
Knowetop Primary School

Rugby

I see 21 men or women on the field.
I feel excited and nervous as I train for the match.
I hear my coach shouting at us to do it right.
And I smell the fear of the other team as they get ready.

I see the man I am about to tackle
And the ball in his hands.
I feel my leg bleeding and hurting.
I hear my teammates running around me
And shouting to pass the ball.
I smell the mud under my feet.

I see my teammates jumping and celebrating
And my opponents walking away in a mood.
I feel ecstatic after winning the match.
I hear my coach shouting, 'Well done!'
I smell the victory of my teammates and I.

Fraser Joyce (11)
Knowetop Primary School

The Circus

The circus is an exciting place
It always gives me a happy face.
The ringmaster is always full of glee
It's a shame he always has to flee.
The tightrope walkers concentrate
It's a wonder they don't dehydrate.
The gymnasts always do their thing
Perfect stunts in the small ring.
The stupid clowns are always silly
With their costumes big and frilly.
The magicians fool everyone
Even when they've begun and done.
The lion tamer is very brave
Even when they don't have a slave.
So there is the circus for you
I hope you go to the circus too!

Rebekah Wilson (11)
Knowetop Primary School

My Rabbit

My rabbit's name is Jess
I nearly called her Bess.
Her hutch is nice and cosy
And she is very nosy.

I feed her before I go to school
She must always have water, that's a rule.
I miss her when I sit in class
Wondering if she is eating grass.

My dad's going to build a run
When the summer is going to come.
Jess and I have become good friends
And I hope her life never ends.

Susan Cunningham (10)
Knowetop Primary School

Feelings

Sometimes I'm happy
Sometimes I'm sad
Sometimes I'm yappy
Sometimes I'm mad

Sometimes I'm chirpy
Sometimes I'm fazed
Sometimes I'm perky
Sometimes I'm dazed

Sometimes I'm afraid
Sometimes I'm muddled
Sometimes I'm enraged
Sometimes I'm puzzled

These are my feelings
Good or bad
I can't change them
But hey I'm glad.

Tommy McGlynn (11)
Knowetop Primary School

Up In The Hills

Up in the hills far, far away,
I walked through the grass, wanting to play
there was no one there except for me,
I was feeling depressed, I don't know why
I actually felt I was going to cry.

I kept on walking by myself,
but then I stopped and looked,
over the hills and down to the ground,
there were flickering lights surrounding the houses
and then a slight breeze came blowing
through my long brown hair.

All of a sudden my depressed feelings
drifted away and then I felt happy again.

Maria Kennedy (11)
Knowetop Primary School

The Way My Teacher Looks

Mrs Monotonous storms through the hall,
High heels on all day,
As if she's going to war,
I wish she would go away!

I don't like her much,
She chases us all day,
But there isn't time to play,
When she's coming your way!

She turns beetroot red,
She gives us the whip,
But then we have to dip,
If she happens to slip!

She calls us all *Dear,*
But if we get too near,
Or if we start to swear,
She pulls out her hair!

Ashley Baird (11)
Knowetop Primary School

My Gran

My gran has steely-grey hair
She has pretty sky-blue eyes
My gran has a strange but wonderful hobby
She collects china houses
Which she keeps in a display cabinet.

My gran likes to cook
Out of her wonderful recipe book
Her food is always scrumptious
And I can never wait to be fed
Though I have to!

My gran is always cleaning up
The mess I leave lying
Her house always smells of pretty pink flowers
That eventually is tidy
Till I mess it up again!

My gran is forever sleeping
That drives my papa mad
My gran cannot sleep at night
And it serves her right
She should go into respite!

Claire Smith (11)
Knowetop Primary School

What's The Point In Homework?

What's the point in homework?
There isn't one if you think.
All that science, maths and English,
It's a waste of paper and ink.

'I'd rather be walking the dogs,
Or watching the telly inside,
I'd rather be out with my friends,
Than be doing my homework,' I cried.

My teacher says if I do my homework,
I'll pass my exams in high school,
But I want to play my guitar,
Doing your homework's not cool.

Whoever invented homework,
Wasn't thinking of people like me,
I'd rather be riding my bike
Or be playing up in a tree.

I'll put my homework in the bin,
Or wash it down the sink.
What's the point in homework,
There isn't one if you think.

Catriona Walker (11)
Knowetop Primary School

Molly Brown

Poor little Molly Brown
Was the new kid in town
She didn't know anyone's names
And they wouldn't let her play their games.
She was sitting all alone
When she saw a wishing stone
It was sparkling on the ground
And she couldn't believe what she'd found.
'Molly, Molly do you want to play?'
This has been a brilliant day.
Everyone wanted her to be their friend
She didn't want this day to end
Soon she woke up from her dream
Oh what does this mean
Had she really found the stone?
Was she still all alone?
'Molly, Molly come and play,'
So she skipped over happily!

Heather Patterson (11)
Knowetop Primary School

Yetis

Yetis are big, hairy and scary.
Are they real? Nobody knows.
They live all over the place -
(Well, I think so!)
There are many of them:
Bigfoot, Abominable Snowman,
The yellow belly custard yeti.
Some live in caves,
Some live in holes,
Some live in water,
(Well I think so.)

Natalie Wallace (11)
Knowetop Primary School

My Favourite Foods

My favourite foods are tasty and great
My favourite foods are like cheese on a plate
From Indian to Italian to Chinese to rice
From pizza to pasta they're always nice
My favourite foods are simply splendid
My favourite foods are like strawberries blended

My favourite foods are as sticky as jam
My favourite foods are as chewy as ham
My favourite foods are as watered as fish
My favourite foods are like bread on a dish

When I'm in a restaurant I'll always ask
'Can I have some soup in a flask?'
'Waiter, waiter I'll take,
A salad with onions or a tuna steak
These are most of my favourite foods
To me, they're like worthy goods.

Jack Cunningham (11)
Knowetop Primary School

Spring

Rosy apples,
Green leaves,
Clear blue skies,
Fluffy clouds,
New baby lambs,
New flowers growing,
Lots of animals awake from hibernation.
Now the fields are fresh and green
Lots of birds come back by spring.
Good day spring,
Goodnight winter.

Laura Farrell (11)
Knowetop Primary School

Oh Homework! Oh Homework!

Oh homework, oh homework, why do you exist?
I hate you so much that I'll hit you with my fist,
I would prefer to fight with my brothers or talk to others,
Or play in the park well after dark,
Or even go for a walk with my dog,
But most of all I would prefer to go for a jog!

Well, I suppose that you are not that bad,
I mean, there must be a reason for you!
But I would prefer to be in my bed right now,
With a temperature and the flu!

Oh homework, oh homework, we don't just get on,
I hope that tomorrow you will be gone
But I know that this will not come true,
You see, that's just the difference between me and you!

Emily Thomson (11)
Knowetop Primary School

My Dog Teenie

My dog Teenie is small and weenie,
When she is sleepy she looks cute and dreamy.

When she was a puppy,
She was not very fluffy.

When she eats vindaloo,
She causes a big hullabaloo.

At the park she likes to bark at strangers,
When she thinks that we're in danger.

When the postman is doing his round,
Teenie barks and he drops his letters on the ground.

Sometimes naughty, sometimes good,
She is never in a mood,
She is always nice and tame,
And I'll always love her just the same.

Hannah Yates (11)
Knowetop Primary School

My Dog Fred

My dog Fred is a Labrador cross
That likes to get into trouble,
When we take him for a walk
He likes to jump up on people.

While he was out in the garden
The rain began to fall,
The grass became all muddy
As Fred ran over it all.

His paws made a mess on the lino
As he skidded across the floor,
By the time my mother said, 'Bath time!'
He had bolted out the door.

One day he broke a vase
Which was completely accidental,
Then my mother said to me
That he was totally mental.

When it's time to go to bed
He lies down in his basket,
Then I think of the things he's done
It's as if he's trying to mask it.

Emma Cartwright (11)
Knowetop Primary School

My Group

In my class we sit in groups,
We work all day and play with hoops.
I'd like to introduce you to,
My friends, so here we go, woo hoo!

They call my friend the rainbow kid,
She's the best friend a kid could get
And Rebekah sitting next to her,
Is the ruler of the net.

Then Matthew right beside her,
His nickname being Pele,
Is one of the best at football,
Because he really gives it welly.

Then Ryan who sits beside him,
Is the maddest of them all,
I have to sit beside him,
So you can see I have a ball!

Well that's my group,
So there you go,
If you want to see,
It ain't no show!

Yvonne Milne (11)
Knowetop Primary School

Season

Spring is a wonderful season
because the flowers come out,
the trees become beautiful with green leaves,
the sun shines on everybody.
The flowers become pink, green, orange, yellow and red,
all different kinds of colours.

Summer is wonderful too,
it has flowers growing, sun shining
and the grass is pure green,
flowers are still as colourful as ever,
the trees are as wonderful as ever too.

Autumn is okay, the leaves fall off,
they all lie on the ground.
Flowers all die,
the birds all fly away for the winter
so that they can get warmth.

Winter is brilliant because there is snow.
Oh and you can play in the snow
all day and all night,
when you come in you are soaked!

Ross Thomson (11)
Knowetop Primary School

Why, Why?

Why can't I do this?
Why can't I do that?
Why can't I do all the things I see
On TV
And in the paper?
Maybe I will do it later.
I'll run about and have some fun
In the rain and in the sun.

I used to play all the games,
Play with toys and play with planes.
That was long ago,
Now I can't even show.

Now the fun in the sun has passed
Wow! It has gone so fast.
Now I hate the rain and hate sun,
And for this old man there will be no more fun.

Gary McLaughlan (11)
Knowetop Primary School

The Flying Pie

I looked up to the sky
and then I saw a pie.
The pie flew down, fell flat on es heed
and then it sadly died.

The pie has risen fae the deed
an' slapped me right across da heed.
So a hitm way oa metal pole
an' then a swalled 'im
oh so whole!

Deane Brown (11)
Knowetop Primary School

The Difference Between The Weather And A Woman

The weather is like a woman,
unpredictable and fickle.
If you get stuck in a snowstorm,
then you're in a pickle.

Weather is like a woman,
it can be so calm and sunny,
just like a woman when
she has got plenty of money.

Weather is like a woman
when the storms and winds do blast,
you hear her ranting and raving when
my papa drives the car too fast!

The weather is like a woman,
when the sun comes out today,
she dons her bikini
in the garden always, all day.

Charlotte Boyd (11)
Knowetop Primary School

Me And Mine

I tidy my room never
If my mum walks in she will shiver
My brother's room is ever so tidy
If I ever see my brothers in a nightie
They won't look so big 'n' mighty
All I ever do is fight with my brother
My family is sick of it, especially my mother.

20 minutes I'm on the phone
On my mobile I like to have a cool tone
Maybe even some of my bling
I give my shoes a bright black shine
Using extracted juice from lime.

Jennifer Harris (11)
Knowetop Primary School

The Cat

The cat was very fat,
It sat lazily on the mat,
It saw a wee rat.

It chased the rat,
But slipped on the mat,
It hit a table and went splat.

The rat laughed at the cat,
The owner took the cat
And sat him on the mat.

The cat and rat played tig,
But the cat fell over a twig,
The rat said, 'You're het,'
But the cat went to the vet.

The cat was now dead,
Because the rat hit him on the head.
He hit him with a brick,
And clobbered him with a stick,
So, no more Mr Cat.

David Kirkwood (11)
Knowetop Primary School

The Snowstorm

Snow is crashing
on the ground
and tickling me.
Snowflakes twirling around
in the sky,
snow and hailstones
coming fast,
hitting my face.
I can hear wind whistling
and trees rustling.

Aaron Lee (8)
Netherburn Primary School

The Snowstorm

Snowflakes twirling.
Trees waving and spinning,
snow falling from the sky
blown by the wind.
The wind is strong
and the snow is swirling, dancing,
the trees are shaking,
the wind is blowing.

Gerry McGuinness (7)
Netherburn Primary School

The Snowstorm

Snowflakes twisting all around,
in the wind through the night,
flying in the heavy wind.
Snowflakes tickling on my face,
flying through the night.
Trees blowing in the park,
children laughing, some crying.

Lee Waugh (9)
Netherburn Primary School

The Snowstorm

Snowflakes falling and dancing
in the wind,
snowflakes tickling very softly,
snow falling,
blistering winds whistling
and church bells ringing
in the cold air.

Jack Kennedy (8)
Netherburn Primary School

The Snowstorm

Snowflakes twirling, dancing in the wind,
scurrying quickly to the ground
melting down my neck
going as fast as a racing greyhound.

Snowflakes tickling
and making me shiver
going gently like a river
making me feel cold and miserable.

Trees rustling, wind whistling,
owls hooting, cars revving,
children laughing.

Matthew Young (8)
Netherburn Primary School

The Snowstorm

Snow rustling, bushes waving,
snow all around me,
tickling me.

Snow falling towards me,
falling on my head and arms,
cars sliding on the road.

Children shouting,
footsteps on the snow,
wind whistling in the trees.

Courtney Lee (8)
Netherburn Primary School

The Snowstorm

Snowflakes spinning
and dancing all around me,
blown by the wind
and falling.

Snowflakes softly
tapping me on the shoe,
cold people
going to their homes.

Trees whistling and owls hooting,
children shouting and shivering,
church bells ringing
through the night.

Aidan Kelly (8)
Netherburn Primary School

The Snowstorm

Snow rustling, bushes waving,
Trees blowing all around,
Snow swirling everywhere,
Snow falling towards me
Heavily, softly on my body,
Head and arms too.

Cars sliding,
Bells ringing,
Children shouting,
Filled with joy,
Footsteps in the snow.

Alex Kelly (7)
Netherburn Primary School

The Snowstorm

Snowflakes twirling,
dancing all around me,
falling heavily.
White spinning, swirling, scurrying.

Snowflakes tickling
your face softly,
thinking about
a nice warm fire.

Trees rustling,
footsteps crunching on the hill.
Church bells ringing,
children playing.

Maxine Armstrong (7)
Netherburn Primary School

The Snowstorm

Snowflakes spinning all around me,
Trees blowing everywhere,
Snow everywhere.

Snow hitting off my face,
Feeling myself shivering,
Soft snow on my face,
Trees rustling,
Wind whirling
Church bells ringing,
The wind blowing.

Kevin Clilverd (8)
Netherburn Primary School

Fairies And Pixies - My Fantasy

Fairies and pixies flying around
Fairies found some flowers
Werewolves and dragons, run for your life
Don't stop. Keep running,
If you don't you'll be knifed with a paw of knives.

Fairies and pixies still flying away
To a very special bay,
I'll say you're lucky, you got away.
Look, a mermaid, her name is Kay
And another called Ray.
'Hello pixies,' one says,
'Hello fairies,' another says.
'Where are we?' a pixie says.
'You're at the special bay
But without a name.'

'Fairies and pixies, why are you here?'
'Oh you dear, we're here because we were driven away.
Please can we stay?'
'No, you can't stay because you don't belong.'
'Oh but we've got a long way to go and we're so slow at flying.'

'Fairies and pixies we must go back to our homeland,
Flying and flying, no going back now.
We're home! We're home! Come on, let's go in!'

'Fairies and pixies, fairies and pixies, do be safe
And do have faith! And you'd better stay
In my fantasy world.'

Rachel Marshall (10)
New Stevenston Primary School

Pets At Home

Pets, pets, pets, my pet rabbit, his name is Alven,
his colour is a charcoal grey and he's 11 months old.
He enjoys getting scrubbed, stroked and cuddled,
he likes playing with me in the house.

He runs about the back garden in his free time,
he enjoys eating stuff like carrots, cabbage, turnip, crisps
                                               and Mars bars.
he drinks water, flavoured water and cola,
he likes where the sun shines brightly in his hut,
no matter what, he'll always be my little bud.

He likes going for walks when he growls and moans
but when he gets back, he always takes a nap,
but the best part is he's always there for me
because he's my bestest friend ever.
No matter what, I will never let go of him.
He's my best friend ever.

Lee Erwin (10)
New Stevenston Primary School

My Best Friend, Ben!

My dog, Ben, is always in trouble,
Just like me - the exact double!
Always chewing slippers, always on the run,
He likes to play tuggy and loves playing with everyone,
He likes to give kisses, he always jumps up for a cuddle
And he cannot miss a puddle!
He's small and cute,
Soft and patchy, but I can't press a button and put him on mute.
Ben is my buddy, I'm never alone -
If he leaves me, I'll moan and moan,
He likes to go for walks out in the rain,
He gets very wet but I'll never complain.
So now I've told you about my little best friend.

Rachel Anderson (10)
New Stevenston Primary School

Seasons

Spring

In spring you can see baby birds in the trees,
just hatched and very young.
You start to see bulbs rising from the ground.
On top of the trees you start to see buds.

Summer

In the summer you can see the golden sunshine very brightly,
playing football is such a delight.
Seashells pure white, never rainy, quite a delight.

Autumn

In the autumn the leaves start to fall from the trees,
what a lovely sight to see, some trees have no leaves,
some trees have some leaves and some trees have a lot of leaves.

Winter

In the winter everything is white, no leaves, only white trees.
All the birds have flown down south.
Snowmen are getting built and there are a lot of snowball fights
and, the best of all, it's *Christmas time!*

Colin Craig (10)
New Stevenston Primary School

My Favourite Thing

My favourite thing is my computer,
The game I play is 'The Lord Of The Rings Battle For Middle-Earth'.
I play online all the time,
I can't help but stop and stare.
Every day I start to play,
It's my favourite thing, I can't stop playing,
Although I still need to play, I have to work all through the day.
I think about it all through school time,
I can't wait until it's fully mine.

Andrew Howieson (10)
New Stevenston Primary School

Four Seasons

My favourite season is autumn,
I like it because I can see the leaves
That are as red as a blazing fire.
I like the trees that are as bare as a bone.

This is a season that is exciting
because of the sky that shines on the Atlantic Ocean,
and I like it another way.
I like it because of all the flowers
that bloom like an enormous forest.

This is a season that is hot,
this is when trees get leaves.
This is a season that I like
because it is my birthday.

I really like this season
because of the white snow
and because it is Christmas,
we can make snowmen and snow angels.

Stevenlee Codona (10)
New Stevenston Primary School

My Imaginary Friend

Last month I thought of an imaginary friend,
His name is Trusty the dog.
Trusty lives in the imaginary world,
He has parents and a little brother,
He's a mongrel with big ears.

His face is like a dog with an alien's body,
He's a talented dog and he likes to jog.
He's my best friend, my mongrel dog.
We go for walks beside the sea,
He likes swimming and he likes me.

Rachel Ferguson (10)
New Stevenston Primary School

A Place In My Mind

In my mind I think of a lot but I know what I want,
I have my own boat and plasma TV which cost a lot of money.
I have five bunk beds for a billionaire
and a helicopter to fly through the air.
I also have jewellery which is known as bling,
it has a big shine but is worth more than a dime.
I have 10 guard dogs to surround my mansion,
you need a pass to get by them.
I get a Dairy Milk delivery every week
and that means unlimited chocolate.
I have a lot of clothes, designer for most,
also some hair gel that is a must
and with all these things, this is my place
and it's got a place in my mind.

Colin Mulvaney (10)
New Stevenston Primary School

Seasons

This is a poem about seasons
and I wrote it for lots of reasons.
Let's start with some spring,
it has eggs, bunnies and flowers.

Next here's summer, it's a good time
because we can go outside and have water fights,
but when it's bedtime we turn off our lights.

But what about autumn? That's a start.
I think you are really going to love this part,
it's about Hallowe'en, time for trick or treat,
all the doors could be filled with spooky fiends.

Oh we must not forget winter, it may be cold, frosty, windy,
but it's the season of Christmas
with presents and the birth of Jesus.

Nicole Cowan (10)
New Stevenston Primary School

A Very Close Friend

Rebecca

My friend, Rebecca, loves her teddy bear,
She does not care if it begins to wear.

Rebecca likes playing football
Even though she is *not* very tall.

Rebecca is very pretty
She is not scared, always witty.

I love playing with her, she is fun,
We love playing together in the sun.

Her eyes are muddy green,
She is never mean.

So this is the poem, this is the end,
Rebecca will always be my best friend.

Nicole Harper (10)
New Stevenston Primary School

My Best Friend

Rebecca

My best friend is very pretty,
she is never scared, always witty,
she is not tall
in fact she's the opposite, she is very small,
she is very smart and into art,
her favourite Simpsons' character is Bart.

She has dark brown hair, muddy green eyes,
and sometimes lies,
she is full of fun
and doesn't like to run,
she doesn't like bright light,
wants to be a vampire so she can bite.

Samantha Sweeney (10)
New Stevenston Primary School

At The Seaside

In the sun, having fun, running about in the water,
Then I came out and tottered about in and out of the sand,

Back into the water and I saw a mermaid with very big fins,
I swam down to get her and there were shells made out of big
                                                    silver tins.

I picked them up, they were a bit hard
And then I went to the mermaid's yard.
I met her blue dog, his name was Daniel,
He was a small springer spaniel.
She said Daniel liked playing with a kite
But he would never ever bite.
We swam out of the sea,
We had chocolate which was free.
I went back to the shore
That I really adore,
I was about to sneeze
When I felt the breeze
I said goodbye
And hoped my mermaid friend would never die.

Stephanie Devlin (10)
New Stevenston Primary School

Make-Believe Poem

Seashore, seashore sitting by the sea,
Gold sand sitting in the hallowed land,
Black seashells smell of salt,
The sparkling sea shines like a diamond on a ring.
Palm trees sway in the sea breeze,
Dolphins swimming up and down
Like a yo-yo in the town.
Fish swimming all around, up and down,
The horizon is down, time to go.

Melissa Cameron (10)
New Stevenston Primary School

What I Feel For My Friend

My dog is called Tara, my dog is a friend,
She's always there when I need her help.
She looks like a fox with her orange locks,
She's so friendly, never hurts anybody,
She's so small, just about the size of a doll,
She sleeps on a bed with her tail waggling,
Sometimes you would think she was sleeping so silently,
I love playing with her,
She is fun,
Her hair is like the golden sun.
I sit and look at her barking away,
Hoping one day she will never ever run away.
I play with her day and night,
Never going to sleep without a clap or a bite,
This is my poem, this is the end,
Tara will always be my friend.

Natasha Smellie (10)
New Stevenston Primary School

The Perfect Pet

The perfect pet for me is cute and cuddly,
It's white and black and it doesn't quack
And is always there when I want it to be.

It cheers me up when I'm down
And he loves running round and round.
He loves to play even when it's rainy.

He loves my family and me very much
And he's such a mutt
We all love him for what he is.

So this is the end and I'll tell you that his name,
Is Robbie and he's my best friend.

Laura Samson (10)
New Stevenston Primary School

My Poem About My Big Friend

Jingle, jingle, jingle, as Zico's chain bobbed up and down,
when he plays he acts like a clown,
when he tries to give you some kisses, he always misses.
He is a big Rottweiler but is just a big friend,
he would not hurt anyone any day,
when he tries to give kisses I would keep far away.
His little stump, cute and curled,
I would not give him away for the world
He is always happy but never yappy
and does not need a nappy.
When he was seven weeks old,
he did not do what he was told.
He is very young with a very long tongue,
he has giant paws and teeth like saws.
My big friend does not mind going to the vets
as long as there are other pets.
Every day he goes a different way on his big, long walks.

Billy Lang (10)
New Stevenston Primary School

My Imaginary World

My imaginary world would be all for me,
There would be flowers, designer clothes and chocolate would be free!
There would be fairies, elves and sparkling lights,
Damsels in distress and heroic knights.
I would have my own shopping centre with designer shops galore,
TVs, flowers and much, much more.
Mermaids and pixies would be best friends,
Werewolves and toads would set their own trends.
I would have two ponies and a unicorn as my pets,
A ballerina would be my next-door neighbour, the one that I met.
But I think this world is sort of okay,
I'm sure it'll be fine if it stays that way.

Chloe McMenemy (10)
New Stevenston Primary School

Playground Poet

Playground, playground, lovely and clean,
and every child's happy
apart from the ones who have been naughty or bad.
You can play all sorts of games,
ground, ground, solid as a rock,
fall, fall, it might be sore.
Round the clock working my hands,
playing in goal, over me the ball might go,
under my legs the ball might go,
never ever miss a shot.
Diving, diving on the ground,
lumps and bumps on my body,
scratches and grazes everywhere,
really, really hard surface,
chases, chases, running about like crazy.
The best place on Earth is our playground.

Lee Knox (10)
New Stevenston Primary School

My Pet Dog

When I got my puppy
he was so cute.
He was so soft and fluffy,
my little puppy.
Now he is older, he is 3,
he is playful, he plays with me.
He is a Labrador, so sweet,
he always lies by the heat.
He's so faithful, loyal and true,
I love him so much.
His ears are soft and neat,
he has got lots of fur
and loves to chase the cats that purr.
He is so very kind and he loves to find.
He's my sweet little puppy, Junior.

Donnamarie McCusker (10)
New Stevenston Primary School

My Dreamland

In my dreamland anything can happen,
Dogs can talk and cats start rapping.
I can fly in the sky with the wind in my face,
Not on a broomstick, least not in this case.

I can swim and breathe in the cool, cool water
And go back in time to when I began to totter.
I live in the castle so huge and big,
Run through the forest and break every twig.

I run along on the hot desert sand,
Go to Hogwarts, let HP lend a hand.
Learning how to cast spells and make potions,
Put on lots of luxurious lotions.

Walk down the celebrity red carpet,
Buy lots of foods from a small French market.
Play with a full on rock 'n' roll band,
Not in reality, but in my dreamland.

Rebecca Ryce (10)
New Stevenston Primary School

The Bobby Poem

Bobby, he's a dog called a Yorkshire Terrier,
He is cute, he is sweet,
He likes Coco Pops and chocolate buttons
And he loves taking baths.

Bobby loves walks and loves to play with me,
But sometimes barks at the postman
And other people who come to my house
When they knock on the door.

Bobby loves to come upstairs and sleep with me,
And likes to play with the football with me,
And likes to come on the couch with me
When I'm watching TV.

Fiona Bruce (10)
New Stevenston Primary School

My Perfect House

My perfect house would be neat and tidy,
It would be in Barbados where the sun shines brightly,
It would smell really nice, as lovely as a rose,
It would be like a big mansion and that's how it goes.

My room would be as lilac as lavender,
It would have posters on the wall with a McFly calendar,
I would have a four-poster bed with colourful cushions everywhere,
I would also have a fluffy rug made of real animal hair.

The kitchen would have a round glass table
And out of the window a horse in its stable.

The garden would have a swimming pool
With water sparkling in the sun like a blue lagoon.
My house would obviously be number one,
After all, who wouldn't want a house in the sun?

Lynsey McMenemy (10)
New Stevenston Primary School

Fairies And Pixies

Fairies flying all around,
Pixies always on the ground,
Lots of people come to stay
So they have to get out of the way.
Fairies and pixies get up to mischief,
They steal the people's handkerchiefs.
The people look confused,
They have to be excused.
The fairies and pixies laugh very loudly,
The rest of the fairies look at them proudly.
Fairies and pixies hide in their tree house,
Their neighbour is a little field mouse.
Every four years they disappear
Preparing for another year.
Now my poem has come to an end,
But the fairies and pixies are still my friends.

Amanda Galloway (10)
New Stevenston Primary School

In My Fantasy Land

In my fantasy land there are dragons and knights,
An enchanted forest with fairy lights,
Mermaids sitting in a blue lagoon,
Werewolves howling at the moon,
A secret cove filled with precious stones
And fossils of ancient dinosaur bones.
Elves and pixies everywhere,
That I always stop and stare.
Unicorns roam anywhere they like,
The one that I think of, his name is Spike,
Heroes brave and heroes true,
Kills the things that come to eat you.
A giants' town far, far away,
Some of the giant children come to play.
Cyclops and trolls hide in the mountains,
Hidden by an enormous fountain.
Going for a sail out on a boat,
Remember to bring an overcoat.
The king of the sea will bring a storm,
So we need to keep nice and warm.
In the enchanted forest there are talking trees
Quicksand if you step in it you are up to your knees.
Fairies wearing tutu skirts,
Penguins wearing gentlemen's shirts.
A sea monster pops out of the sea
On a scary dark night, tu-whit, tu-whee.
My daydream is fading, pink clouds appear,
I wake up in reality, oh no, oh dear.
I suppose it's OK, I suppose it's alright,
It should be OK, because this is my life.

Jennifer Reid (10)
New Stevenston Primary School

A Place In The Clouds

Walking through a world, forget all your fears,
Forget all your troubles that have been bothering you for years.
With worries off your shoulders you feel so light,
Looking at the friendly faces shining so bright.

Come with me, come and see, a wonderful land,
With shallow water, a gentle breeze and golden sand.
Where the sun always shines and the moon always beams,
This place is beyond your wildest dreams!

Where white horses leap upon the waves
And dolphins swim in the waters,
Where rabbits can leap, and no one can weep,
Where the lights shine so bright, even at night.
The choir sing their songs with voices as sweet as chocolate,
The clouds are as soft as candyfloss,
The rivers flow as runny as sauce.

Could you ever imagine a place so wonderful?
Could you ever imagine a place so colourful?

Rachael Kelly (10)
New Stevenston Primary School

My Brother Jack

I had a little brother called Jack,
Who went to the park,
But didn't come back.

He climbed trees and swam all day,
Wearing a leopard skin
To keep the cold away.

One year later he came back,
Tall and handsome
And munching a Big Mac.

Amy Townsley (10)
Our Lady & St Francis Primary School

Haunted Mansion

A haunted mansion is a scary place,
So I just went and washed my face.
'Let's make toast,' someone said,
But they couldn't find any bread.

Candles everywhere, a strange light,
First it was dark, then it was bright.
Suddenly I heard a *crash*,
Because the staircase had turned into ash.

I had spoiled their summer ball,
But it wasn't my fault at all.
They attacked me - I let out a scream,
I woke up shaking, phew it was just a dream.

Alisha Blair (10)
Our Lady & St Francis Primary School

Ben

Ben is my lovely, little, brown dog,
When we got him he behaved like a frog.
Jumping here, jumping there,
Bouncing about without a care.

He searched the house looking for a shoe,
Picking the colour he'd like to chew.
When he found one, he'd lie on his cover,
Tear it to pieces, then look for another.

Day is done, time for bed,
He sleeps in the corner,
Paws covering his head.

Cheryl Bradley (10)
Our Lady & St Francis Primary School

World War II

On September the 3rd
War was declared,
Laughter ceased,
Anger flared.

Bombs dropping from planes,
All running scared,
Hitler was hated,
Churchill revered.

Living on rations
Wasn't so good,
So we grow a patch
For some extra food.

ID and gas masks,
Countries in need,
All this because
Of one man's greed.

Hiding in shelters,
We sit and wait,
When will this end?
Where lies our fate?

Our men off fighting
On foreign ground,
Deliver them Lord,
All safe and sound.

Home front protecting
At our front doors,
Murdering Nazis
Like rampaging boars.

Nearing to an end,
Almost in sight,
Come on our boys
Win the last fight.

Six years gone now,
All in the past,
The world at peace,
Liberty at last!

Monica Bonham (11)
Our Lady & St Francis Primary School

Winter Sound

It's snowing, it's snowing during the night,
Giving drivers a nasty fright.
The sun comes up and it turns to slush,
So I sweep it away with a heavy brush.
I sprinkle salt on the ground,
Oh! how I love that winter sound.

The wind is strong and the trees are blowing,
Sheep bleat while the cattle are lowing.
Flowers are covered with ice and snow,
But I'm in the house watching the fire glow.
I look out the window and guess what I see?
A bear growling behind the apple tree.

I return from school and Mum gives me a hug,
While we drink tea from a latte mug.
By the fire I sit with my mum,
While Dad's upstairs banging a drum.
Then I hear next-door's howling hound,
Oh! how I love that winter sound.

Stephanie Caldow (9)
Our Lady & St Francis Primary School

Molly

Molly is my pet, a big fluffy cat,
I can tell you she's all of that.
She lies in the living room, then goes out the door,
Brings back a mouse and boy does Mum roar.

Molly is white with big blue eyes
And there on the window sill she lies.
She gazes at me day and night,
Her eyes glisten like the stars so bright.

Nicola Reilly (10)
Our Lady & St Francis Primary School

The Field Mouse

In the dark forest there was a house,
All that lived there was a field mouse.
Up and down the stairs he would run,
Running around, having such fun.

At dinner time he would eat,
His favourite meal, oats and wheat.
When it's time for sleep, upstairs he goes,
Into bed for a midnight doze.

Mobeen Aftab (10)
Our Lady & St Francis Primary School

I Don't Know

I can't write a poem,
'Cause I don't know what to write.
I've thought so hard
All through the night.

I woke up this morning,
I looked a terrible sight.
And you'll never guess what
I still don't know what to write.

Melissa Austin (10)
Our Lady & St Francis Primary School

Cats

Cats are cuddly,
Cats are cute,
Fascinated with my foot.

They can jump
And play all day,
And they watch as I walk away.

I would love
To play with you,
But you make me go achoo, achoo!

Katie McShane (10)
Our Lady & St Francis Primary School

Countries

France and Ireland,
Far away from Thailand,
In fact, across the sea.
Both of them are fun,
With plenty of sun,
But Scotland is the land for me.

Joseph Wilson (10)
Our Lady & St Francis Primary School

Sport

My favourite sport is football,
I play it all the time,
But if I try to play indoors,
Mum begins to whine.

My second favourite one is golf,
I play it with my dad.
He tries to teach me all he knows,
It's a pity he's so bad.

Ryan Clark (10)
Our Lady & St Francis Primary School

Tae Ma Dug Dodger

Wee black and cheeky, artful nutter,
Ye won't eat yer toast without any butter.

Mither treats ye like a baby,
Faither'll take ye tae a dug home, maybe.

Open the door and off ye run,
Dodgin' and divin', lookin' for fun.

It's an awfy hassle gettin' ye back,
If ye don't come at once, ye'll get a smack.

Doon Strathy we went oot a walkin',
To all the other dugs, yer talkin'.

Exhausted and hungry, back to Carfin,
No more dodgin' now . . . we'll have a quiet night in.

Kevin Connelly (10)
Our Lady & St Francis Primary School

My Dog Toby

My dog Toby is black and white,
When he was little
He barked through the night.
But now he is older
He just wants to play,
So I take him outside
For walks every day.

My dog Toby was very small,
But now he is big and very tall.
He loves to drink water
And eat doggy food.
He's my best friend
And I treat him good.

Thomas Sinnott (10)
Our Lady & St Francis Primary School

A Lava Lamp

A lava lamp is good to keep,
It certainly helps me to sleep,
To me it's such a beautiful sight,
Giving off a glowing light.

You can get pink, blue, purple and red,
Or you can choose orange instead.
It really is only melted wax,
But it will help you to relax.

Hayley Morrison (9)
Our Lady & St Francis Primary School

Ladybird, Ladybird

Ladybird, ladybird will you stay
Here in my garden if that's OK?

You can live in my shed
And make yourself a cosy bed.

I think you're cute and small,
You won't be any bother at all.

John Paul Devlin (10)
Our Lady & St Francis Primary School

My Dog Kim

My dog Kim,
Is fat so I call her Slim.

She's black and hairy,
That makes her look scary.

She's soft and gentle,
But very temperamental.

John Joe Curran (9)
Our Lady & St Francis Primary School

A Dog Called Jim

I had a dog, his name was Jim
And I was very proud of him.
With one eye blue, the other brown,
The strangest dog in all the town.

I took him for a walk one day,
He slipped the leash and ran away.
Down to the river bank,
Jumped in and slowly sank.

He floated to the top once more
And struck out bravely for the shore.
Trying to get dry was such a pain,
So he jumped in again.

Ryan Watson (10)
Our Lady & St Francis Primary School

Snow

Snowflakes fall from the sky,
As white candyfloss clouds go by.

I see snow falling on the ground,
Looks like sherbet sparkling around.

Trees are frosted lollipops,
Stars are glittering above the shops.

A dove's nest is made of crystal,
Icicles hang from my house window.

Snow is such a beautiful thing,
As beautiful as a bird's wing.

Jennifer Fallon (9)
Our Lady & St Francis Primary School

Snow

Snow is wonderful that's what I say,
So please dress warmly then come out to play.
Snowflakes fall from the sky,
I feel sorry for the firefly,
Having to fly around at night,
So fly in the morning when it's bright.
Even though it is very cold,
It's a mystery still untold.
So drink from your cup of tea,
Let snowdrops lie there, let them be.
Blizzards come and I despise that,
So hide away if you're a cat.
I know snow goes away,
But I wish it was here to stay.
So be careful when you drive your car,
Watch out for that glowing star.
Don't give little robins a fright,
Together with snow they make a beautiful sight.

Hayleigh Kemp (9)
Our Lady & St Francis Primary School

Snow

Snow, snow,
Wonderful snowflakes
Spinning down,
Gathering together
To make a white carpet.
Spoiled by footprints,
As the children
Build a snowman
And play snowball fights.
I love snow.

Nadia Al Murshedy (9)
Our Lady & St Francis Primary School

Snow

Snow is wonderful,
Snow is bright,
Banishing the darkness
With its glowing light,
Fluffy candy clouds go by
Like ice mints hanging in the sky.

The snow is very cold,
So your layers must be thick,
Because if you don't
You will end up sick,
I love the snow, it's so much fun,
I hope it doesn't melt in the sun.

Aimee Crawford (9)
Our Lady & St Francis Primary School

Snow

Today it is snowing,
My favourite time of the year.
Everyone comes out to play,
'Frosty's here,' they cry out,
As the blizzard comes.
Snowflakes fall
Like small meteors,
Covering the footprints
On the white carpet.
The crystal carpet
Glitters in my eye,
As I struggle home
On the frosty road.

Rebecca Hart (9)
Our Lady & St Francis Primary School

Superheroes

Superheroes, superheroes tall and muscular,
Bad guys, bad guys should be much nicer.
Batman and Superman they're in the past,
Dash and the Flash . . . boy can they run fast.
Spider-Man, Spider-Man he's so good,
He became a superhero in his childhood.
Some supers fly, some ride in a car,
But Dash out of 'The Incredibles' can run very far.
Daredevil, Daredevil, he may be blind,
A great superhero . . . one of a kind.

Daniel Cairney & Christopher Finlay (9)
Our Lady & St Francis Primary School

I Like Football

I like football
You kick around a ball
Try to stay on your feet
And try not to fall.

I'm running down the side line
Taking some knocks
I dodge the defence
And score in the box.

Dean Stewart (10)
Our Lady & St Francis Primary School

Snow

It's a blizzard outside,
As children have snowball fights.
The moon gives off a silver light,
As snowflakes float down.
They lie peacefully on the ground,
Until Jack Frost comes.

Nicole Jaques (9)
Our Lady & St Francis Primary School

Snow

Snow is falling heavily tonight,
Nothing you can do,
To stop it.

Looks great,
But it's a
Destructive blizzard.
Spreading,
A huge white carpet,
All over town.
So fast,
I thought the stars were falling
From the sky.

Now it is making snow mountains,
No escape
From your homes.

Dylan Baxendale (9)
Our Lady & St Francis Primary School

Snow

I woke up
And looked out the window,
What a wonderful sight.
Snowflakes falling down,
Creating
A silent sound.

I ran out into the snow,
Had snowball fights
All evening long,
But,
The sun came out,
Melting all my snow.

Andrew Miller (9)
Our Lady & St Francis Primary School

Snow

Snow is beautiful and so bright,
I wish it would snow all night.

Snowflakes tumble from the sky,
We all hope it will lie.

A white covering on the cars
Makes them twinkle like the stars.

Snow is such a beautiful thing,
Sparkling like my mother's ring.

Conor McCormick (9)
Our Lady & St Francis Primary School

Colour

Yellow is a ripe banana,
My lovely blonde hair.

Red is the juicy apple,
My sister's favourite colour.

Blue is the water in the lake,
Dad's favourite shirt.

White are the fluffy sheep,
The snow outside my window.

Eilish Bennett (8)
Our Lady & St Francis Primary School

Snow

Snow
Falls on the ground.
We have snowball fights
Till Jack Frost comes.
But the sun comes out
And melts it all away.

Megan McLean (8)
Our Lady & St Francis Primary School

The Band

I've come all the way from Wishaw
To see my favourite band,
Everybody's watching it
All over God's good land.
I'm so excited I could run around the world,
My teeth were chattering,
I was jumping up and down in my seat,
My juice was splattering.

They took to the stage,
The crowd were cheering.
The stage was lit up more than fire,
No one was jeering
I was jumping so fast and high,
I could see them rocking like legends,
I jumped in the sky and thought I would fly.

The night was over,
We wanted more.
The band was exhausted
Lying on the floor.
They got up and sang one note,
We knew it was an encore.
We went home and went on my karaoke,
I sang and sang until I could sing no more.

Garry Boyle (10)
St Ignatius Primary School, Wishaw

Laughter

Laughter is yellow like the sun shining in the sky,
It smells like the flowers in the summer gardens,
It feels like when you score a goal for the first time,
It tastes like candyfloss at a funfair,
It sounds like a person having good fun,
It looks like a star shining in the dark,
It reminds me of my favourite things.

Megan MacFarlane (10)
St Ignatius Primary School, Wishaw

My Holiday Poetry

The sunburst sky flashed in my eyes
As the water drew nearer.
My dad was taking me to the beach,
I was feeling very eager.
I walked down on the burning sand,
My dad laid out the towels.
I swam through the ocean,
Deep within the bowels.

I had an ice cream later,
The cold cream hit my mouth.
I watched the birds flying,
In winter they fly south.
My dad took us out on our boat,
He pulled us all the way.
I couldn't think of a better way
To finish off the day.

We headed back for home,
I had loads of fun.
I raced Dad back to the apartment,
I never even had to run.
My mum said, 'How was it?'
I answered, 'Take me again.'
I can't wait till tomorrow
For another great day in Spain.

Paul McConville (10)
St Ignatius Primary School, Wishaw

Love

Love is red like a garden full of roses,
It tastes like a hot Sunday roast,
It looks like a summer evening sunset,
It smells like the aroma of roses,
It feels like you're having the time of your life
And it reminds me of music.

Gerald McQuade (10)
St Ignatius Primary School, Wishaw

Tampa

Flying down the highway
It seemed to take forever,
The sun was bursting through the clouds,
It was the best day ever,
We pulled up to the stadium,
It looked like a silver dome
With a sea of people all around,
A long, long way from home.
The baseball flies through the air
Like a soaring bird,
The fans give a cheer.
Yankees hit out the third.
Then we met the Yankees
And got an autographed ball.
They won the game,
It was a time when I was small.

Nicola Rooney (10)
St Ignatius Primary School, Wishaw

Autobiographical Poem

Gerard,
Funny, sporty, friendly, cheerful,
Son of Gerard and Jacki.
I like football,
I feel joyful when I play football.
I need food to stay alive,
I fear clowns because they smile all the time.
In the future I would most like to see a cleaner world.
Live in Wishaw,
Last name Cassidy.

Gerard Cassidy (10)
St Ignatius Primary School, Wishaw

Autobiographical Poem

Kyle,
I am musical, cheerful and friendly,
I am the son of Annette and Sandy Gray.
I like games, football and music.
I feel joyful when it's Christmas.
I need food, music and love from my family.
I give support and amusement.
I fear exams and tests, the dark and heights
And blood and sore pain.
In the future I would like to see the Statue of Liberty.
Resident of Larkhall.
Gray.

Kyle Gray (10)
St Ignatius Primary School, Wishaw

All About Me

Shane,
I am funny, cheerful, musical and friendly.
I like playing football, PE and art,
Son of Wendy and Shane Armstrong.
I feel joyful when it is the summer,
I need family, food, water and friends.
I give respect and love.
I fear water.
In the future I would like to see no war.
My town is Wishaw.
My last name is Armstrong.

Shane Armstrong (11)
St Ignatius Primary School, Wishaw

Laughter

Laughter is yellow like the bright morning sun.
Laughter feels like swimming in the sea.
Laughter smells like lilies in the valley.
Laughter tastes like the pineapple in Capri Sun.
Laughter looks like lavender in the field.
Laughter sounds like a trickle of a burn running into the sea.
Laughter reminds me of my grandad.

Caitlin Glover (10)
St Ignatius Primary School, Wishaw

Laughter

Laughter is yellow like the sunshine,
Laughter tastes like ice cream on your tongue,
Laughter looks like a child on his birthday,
Laughter feels like lying on your bed,
Laughter smells like a candle that's burnt out,
Laughter sounds like a firework going off,
Laughter reminds me of having fun with my friends.

Andrew Watters (10)
St Ignatius Primary School, Wishaw

Fun

Fun is blue like the sky above,
It tastes like the wind in winter,
It smells like morning air on a cold day,
It looks like a funfair,
It feels like riding a bike,
It sounds like people on a roller coaster,
It reminds me of a funfair.

Kealan Hughes (9)
St Ignatius Primary School, Wishaw

My Love For Music

My love for music it's real and true,
I love to play it and hear it through.
I got convinced when I was six,
My mum says it's just like a pick and mix.
You pick a type and try your best,
If it doesn't work through you pick another,
Whether it's rap, jazz or one other.
So I tried out rock, it was really cool,
I play guitar and that is so much fun,
I have a band, its name's Blue
Lightning, we work together with no such fighting.
So there you are my love for music,
I wonder where I'll be in ten years notice.

Barry Hodge (10)
St Ignatius Primary School, Wishaw

Untitled

Leanne, loving, artistic, cheerful and gentle,
Daughter of Sally McMillan and Billy McMillan.
I like art, shopping, hugs, dancing, laughter,
Happiness, Christmas, animals and music.
I feel excited when I am going shopping.
I feel terrified when I am going to do a test.
I need love, water, food, family and respect.
I fear spiders and snakes.
One thing I would like to see in the future is the world.

Leanne McMillan (10)
St Ignatius Primary School, Wishaw

Me

Liam,
I am fast, energetic, lucky and like PS2 games,
I am son of Richard and Karen.
I like art and football,
I feel joyful on Christmas morning,
I need sunshine every day.
I give respect,
I fear some animals.
In the future I would like to see a cure for allergies.
Resident of Wishaw.
McQuade.

Liam McQuade (10)
St Ignatius Primary School, Wishaw

Untitled

Michael,
I am fast, friendly, cheerful and energetic,
Son of Agnes and Kevin,
I like football and climbing.
I feel joyful when I play football,
I need food and water.
I give respect, laughter,
I fear the unknown.
In the future I would like to see the world,
I live in Wishaw.
Larkin.

Michael Larkin (10)
St Ignatius Primary School, Wishaw

Playground

P laying is the best thing that happened to children
L ooking at children having fun
A t playtime you have fun, at playtime you run
Y ou will always have fun in the playground
G oing home is the best but I do not go, I stay and play
R unning round with my friend
O ver and over again
U nder the trees, round the back
N ow it is time to go home
D on't worry I will come back.

Shannon McNeil (10)
St Ignatius Primary School, Wishaw

Playground

P laying is fun when you play too.
L aughing is bright like red roses.
A nd games we play are fun.
Y oung children sometimes get hurt.
G ames we play are good sometimes.
R unning is healthy for you.
O ranges are good to eat.
U learn new games to play.
N aughty children must learn to play nicely.
D octor Dolittle came in the playing ground.

Nikita Reilly (10)
St Ignatius Primary School, Wishaw

Working In The Mill

Hear the poor children screaming and crying as they work.
See the wool and cotton flying all over the wooden floor.
Smell the sweat from my body as I work very hard.
Taste the dust flying into my mouth.
I feel tired, sore and weak as I work very hard all day.

Caitlin Leabody (9)
St Mark's Primary School, Hamilton

A Road Sweeper's Life

Hear the clip-clopping of horses' hooves on the dirty road
And voices of people shouting in the street.
See people chucking water from their window for me to sweep,
Smell the awful manure flooded streets.
Taste the dust from dirty streets in my mouth.
I feel worthless,
I wish a horse and cart would run me over
And end this miserable work.

Mark Russell (11)
St Mark's Primary School, Hamilton

The Chimney Sweep

Hear the fire crackling like a sparkler.
See the bricks crumbling as I wearily climb up the huge chimney.
Smell the smoke rushing from the fire.
Taste the sweat as it pours from my weak body.
I feel overcome with fatigue and exhaustion.

Stephen Queen (10)
St Mark's Primary School, Hamilton

Victorian Mill Worker

Hear the looms crashing together like two hundred drums.
See spindles, too many to count, going back and forth.
Smell the fear in all the workers.
Taste the horrible cotton fibres in my mouth.
I feel anxious that I am next under the loom.

Rebeka Hynes (10)
St Mark's Primary School, Hamilton

The Chimney Sweep

Hear the hot fire burning below,
I hope I don't fall.

See hardly anything because of
The smoke and dust.

Smell the soot coming from my brush
And down my throat.

Taste the horrible soot coming up
And down the chimney.

I feel like I am never going to get
Out of this dirty chimney.

Jenna Dyson (10)
St Mark's Primary School, Hamilton

Houses

H ouses sometimes have swimming pools,
O ur bedroom has bunk beds,
U pstairs there are 2 bathrooms.
S ometimes people have small houses,
E lectricity runs through the wires in our house.
S ometimes people have big and small gardens.

Heather McCafferty (9)
St Mark's Primary School, Hamilton

Houses

H ouses are nice places to live in.
O utside of my house I have a lovely garden.
U pstairs I have 3 bedrooms.
S ome houses are beautiful.
E veryone in my street are my friends but
S ometimes they are not nice.

Lauren Harvey (10)
St Mark's Primary School, Hamilton

Working In The Mill

Hear the looms crashing together
Like 10,000 people screaming at each other.

See the people fighting and shouting
And bawling at each other.

Smell the slimy sweat as they are run off their feet.

Taste the sweat and the cotton in my mouth.

I feel sad, lonely, weak and sleepy
Because I miss my parents,
I *don't* like working.

Hayley Simpson (10)
St Mark's Primary School, Hamilton

Houses

H undreds of people move house every day,
O ne way of finding a house is via the internet.
U tility rooms can have tumble dryers, washing machines
   or even both,
S ome houses can be five hundred years old
   or perhaps even older.
E very one wants good value but
S ometimes they don't get it!

Callum Steven (10)
St Mark's Primary School, Hamilton

Houses

H omes are comfy to everyone.
O ur attic is old and dusty.
U pstairs we have two bathrooms.
S ome houses can be big, others can be small.
E specially in winter my house is cosy.
S omewhere there is a house for everyone.

Emily Hill (10)
St Mark's Primary School, Hamilton

The Scullery Maid

Hear the master shouting, 'Get on with it.'
I think to myself, *I want to die.*

See the birds chirping as I dream about my mum
And jealously watch the master's children playing games.

Smell the sweet smell of fresh clothes
As I hang them up on the washing line.

Taste the fresh bread in the oven
That I made with my own hands.
I feel exhausted and weak as a kitten.

Brogan McKendrick (10)
St Mark's Primary School, Hamilton

Houses

H ouses come in all shapes and sizes.
O ur garden is like Park Head.
U pstairs is where I play with friends.
S ome people have a conservatory.
E verybody is welcome in my house.
S elling your house means you put a
    'For Sale' sign outside your window.

Danielle Barr (9)
St Mark's Primary School, Hamilton

Houses

H ouses are made from different things.
O ur house is so long.
U p above my bedroom is the loft.
S ome houses are so freaky.
E veryone is so friendly in my street but
S oon we are moving and they are going to wave goodbye.

Robert Stone (9)
St Mark's Primary School, Hamilton

Working As A Road Sweeper

Hear the clip-clopping of the horses' hooves
And people muttering to themselves or others.

See people rushing by me
Like a train at lightning speed.

Smell the sweat running down my face
Like a dripping tap that won't stop.

Taste the dust from my clothes
And the dirt from the ground.

I feel worthless because no one thanks me
For sweeping a clear path for them
And exhausted because I have worked all day.

Rachael Feeley (11)
St Mark's Primary School, Hamilton

Love

Love is like the red heart on my bed.
Love sounds like blue water splashing on the beach.
Love is like when you touch colourful feathers
Which are soft and smooth.
Love is like the smell of flowers that smell of perfume.
Love is like the taste of fresh strawberries with cream.

Gemma Leabody (8)
St Mark's Primary School, Hamilton

Anger

Anger is like red vicious snakes ready to bite.
It sounds like banging in my head, drums thumping.
It smells like onions being chopped.
It is spiky like a cactus.
It tastes like red cough medicine.
That's what anger is.

Sean Leabody (8)
St Mark's Primary School, Hamilton

Love

Love is like the sun rising, bright and colourful in the sky.
Love is like the water running, splashing down the waterfall.
Love smells like my mum's lemon perfume she wears going to work.
Love tastes like bubbly strawberry milkshake.
Love feels like velvety fur, it's smooth like my dog.

Mae Reilly (8)
St Mark's Primary School, Hamilton

Houses

H ouses are good to play in.
O utside my garden is a football stadium.
U nder my house is a basement.
S oon I will be moving house.
E verybody is my friend in my street,
S ome people don't like me.

Declan Smith (9)
St Mark's Primary School, Hamilton

Happiness

Happiness looks like colourful, bright flowers.
It sounds like a cat purring on the street.
It smells like your best dinner.
It feels like a nice dog's fur,
It tastes like a red juicy apple.

Kieren McCafferty (8)
St Mark's Primary School, Hamilton

Fun

Fun is a baby's laugh.
Fun is the sound of people singing in church.
Fun is the touch of feathers tickling your back.
Fun is the smell of soapy shampoo on your head.
Fun is the taste of wibbly wobbly jelly.

Chloe Stewart (7)
St Mark's Primary School, Hamilton

Fun

Fun is the fireworks as they shoot in the sky.
It smells like my dad cooking burgers on the barbecue.
It feels warm and cosy when I pat my dog.
It sounds like laughter when I play with my cousins.
It tastes like fizzy sweets exploding in my mouth.

Ruairi Fleming (7)
St Mark's Primary School, Hamilton

Fun

Fun is the fireworks when they burst with stars.
Fun is the fur of a sheep.
Fun is flowers on a sunny day.
Fun is ice cream that tastes like thick snow.
Fun is water splashing and like dolphins splashing in the sea.

Liam Forbes (7)
St Mark's Primary School, Hamilton

Sadness

Sadness is like a baby's cry.
Sadness is the sound of thunder.
Sadness is like touching a frog.
Sadness is like the smell of garlic bread.
Sadness is the taste of toffee.

Colin Henderson (7)
St Mark's Primary School, Hamilton

Love

Love is pink like a Loveheart.
It sounds like a book flipping its pages.
It feels like a rainbow spreading its colours across the sky.
It smells like soapy shampoo on our hair.
It tastes like melted chocolate ice cream.

Jonah Gault (7)
St Mark's Primary School, Hamilton

Happiness

Happiness tastes like chocolate melting in my mouth.
Happiness feels soft like a pony's coat.
Happiness sounds like a cat purring.
Happiness smells like a pink rose.
Happiness looks like cute newborn puppies.

Katie Maguire (7)
St Mark's Primary School, Hamilton

Full Of Love

Love is the sight of beautiful red roses.
Love is the sound of me and my brother Michael having a laugh.
Love is the smell of shampoo that makes my hair smell lovely.
Love is the touch of soft red feathers.
Love is the taste of chocolate.

Kerry McGuckin (7)
St Mark's Primary School, Hamilton

Love

Love is like the beautiful sight of the reflection of the sun.
Love is like the blue shining water flowing from the waterfall.
Love is like soft rose-red silk.
Love is like the dark Bournville chocolate melting on my tongue.
Love is like a gorgeous perfume.

Laura Pollock (8)
St Mark's Primary School, Hamilton

Love

Love is like a beautiful red rose.
Love is like gentle waves rushing through my toes.
Love is like soft velvet.
Love is like lovely flowers.
Love is like delicious chocolate.

Kaitlyn Mitchell (7)
St Mark's Primary School, Hamilton

Love

Love is like a multicoloured rainbow in a sunny,
Beautiful, blue sky without any clouds.
Love smells like a lovely big cake with icing on it.
Love sounds like a quiet cat's purring.
Love feels like smooth silk wrapped around me.
Love tastes like a big bit of chocolate melting in my mouth.

Nicole Harley (8)
St Mark's Primary School, Hamilton

Darkness

Darkness is scary, it is all black like a ghost in the cupboard.
Darkness smells like onions being cooked.
Darkness tastes like thick gooey porridge and baby food.
Darkness feels like squelchy mud and slimy slugs.
Darkness sounds like a ghost screaming.

Omar Khalaf (8)
St Mark's Primary School, Hamilton

Love

Love looks like a lovely red sunset running across the sky.
It sounds like bluebirds singing
And smells like a hot apple pie.
It feels so very wonderful like my dog's fur
And it tastes like frothy strawberry milkshake slipping down my throat.

Lewis Polland (8)
St Mark's Primary School, Hamilton

Love

Love is the sound of a cat purring in the park,
There are lots of cats in the trees.
Love is like seeing a rainbow in the blue sky
When I go out to play.
Love is like the smell of big chocolate muffin
When I come in from football.
Love is like the taste of a big chocolate Galaxy
And a milkshake.
Love is the touch of a smooth little dog.

Jordan Craig (8)
St Mark's Primary School, Hamilton

Love

Love is red like a beautiful sunset across the sky.
Love is like the lovely smell of perfume and flowers.
Love feels like a newborn puppy's fur.
Love tastes like sweet, fruity ice lollies.
Love sounds like water splashing out of a fountain.

Lyndsey Dyson (8)
St Mark's Primary School, Hamilton

Silence

Silence is blue like the peaceful sky.
It sounds quiet like the air outside.
It smells like someone baking a cake.
It feels like a sheep's fur.
It tastes like a big chocolate cake.

Jordan Young (8)
St Mark's Primary School, Hamilton

Hunger

It looks like a dark black empty space sitting on a shelf.
It sounds like a rumbling tummy with nothing in it.
It smells like a lovely smell, like a burger.
It feels like a smooth sausage in the oven.
It tastes like a big juicy burger in my mouth.

Kieran Hartley (8)
St Mark's Primary School, Hamilton

Anger

It feels like a spiky green cactus.
It sounds like hoovering when I'm trying to watch TV.
It looks like a fierce scorpion with a sting in its tail.
It tastes like sour milk on Coco Pops.
It smells like the spray of a skunk.

Martin MacPherson (8)
St Mark's Primary School, Hamilton

Anger

Anger like fire-hot chilli beef burning my tongue.
Anger like big smelly feet marching through the hall.
Anger like grey slimy slugs crawling up my hand.
Anger like a baby crying in the hall.
Anger like black gooey mud in the sandpit.

Daniel Carlton (7)
St Mark's Primary School, Hamilton

Happiness

Happiness is like a blue sky
And flowers fluttering in the breeze.
It tastes like a chocolate cake.
It feels like it's a furry teddy.
It smells like an ice cream cone.
It sounds like a singing dancer.

Declan Doyle (8)
St Mark's Primary School, Hamilton

Frank's Tank

There was a man called Frank
Who invented a wonderful tank
He said it would float
Just like a big boat
But instead it sank.

Daniel McRoberts (9)
St Mary's Primary School, Hamilton

Limerick

There was a young teacher from Spain
She liked to work in the rain
When she got hit
That was it
She never went there again.

Mark Boyle (8)
St Mary's Primary School, Hamilton

The Young Teacher

There was a young teacher from Peru
Who always caught the flu
She took milk and honey
Which made her feel funny
And her nose was runny too.

Megan O'Donnell (8)
St Mary's Primary School, Hamilton

Limerick

There was a young teacher from Greece
She had no money for a piece
She went to buy a bean
And was never again seen
So her friends had to get the police.

Jamie Woodward (8)
St Mary's Primary School, Hamilton

Limerick

There once was a teacher from Spain
Who liked to dance in the rain
But one day she slipped
And hurt her hip
And never was seen again.

Amy Dougan (8)
St Mary's Primary School, Hamilton

There Once Was A Man From Rome

There once was a man from Rome
He slept on a garden gnome
He got such a fright
In the middle of the night
He thought he should have slept in his home.

Scott Agar (8)
St Mary's Primary School, Hamilton

Limerick

There was an old lady from France
Who didn't think she could dance
She went to a ball
She didn't dance at all
She couldn't even prance.

Ainsley Taylor (8)
St Mary's Primary School, Hamilton

Oh Gosh!

There once was a schoolboy called Josh
Who firstly said, 'Oh gosh!'
When he saw his brother Barry
With his girlfriend named Carrie
He remembered he needed a wash.

Lorena Palazzo (8)
St Mary's Primary School, Hamilton

The Wrestling Teacher From Ayr

There once was a young teacher from Ayr
Who loved to wrestle with a bear
She tried it with a crane
She fell in great pain
And now she has long hair.

Matthew Abbott (8)
St Mary's Primary School, Hamilton

Sam And The Flam!

There once was a schoolboy called Sam,
Who only ate eggs, pickle and ham,
He went home from school
And he met an old fool
And then Sam was gone with a *flam!*

Catriona Cherrie (8)
St Mary's Primary School, Hamilton

Dancing In The Rain

There was a young teacher from Spain
Who liked working in the rain
But when it was hot
She decided to stop
'Cause working was really a pain.

Sarah Duddy (8)
St Mary's Primary School, Hamilton

A Boy Called Drew

There once was a boy called Drew
Whose feet just grew and grew
His friends thought it fun
When they watched him run
As his big toe popped out of his shoe.

Lauren Slaven (8)
St Mary's Primary School, Hamilton

Rome Blood

There was an old lady from Rome
Who fell asleep on a gnome!
When she went to bed
She broke her head
So then she had to go home.

Dervla McCormick (8)
St Mary's Primary School, Hamilton

Limericks

There once was a schoolboy called Roy
He ran too fast for a boy
And one day he fell
Right into a well
And a monkey came out with a toy.

Lewis Kemp (8)
St Mary's Primary School, Hamilton

Dancing

Dancing is the best
We welcome all our guests
We think it's very fun
We have merry faces all day long.

All my friends at dancing are very, very good
But only one's the best, my dancing teacher
But she's sometimes in a mood.

She's the best in the world
As anyone can see
She loves all the children
But especially me.

We all love it
Because dancing is amazing, dancing is fun
Dancing is cool and dancing is the one.

Chloe McCluskey (10)
St Mary's Primary School, Hamilton

Football

Football, football, the best game of all
My dad always watches it when drinking alcohol
It is great, it's amazing, it is blazin' with surprise.

In the stadium you can hear the fans roar
As their favourite team score.

Football, football, it's the best
And Celtic beats the rest
No one beats football
Because it's the greatest game of all.

Christopher Szafranek (10)
St Mary's Primary School, Hamilton

Pets

Pets are like your best friends
Except you can never really fall out with them
And they are always around
When you need them most.

Pets are like your family
Except you can never really argue with them
And they are always around
When you need them most.

Pets are the best
They are really cool, they are good to play with
And they are always around
When you need them most.

Pets are lovely, they are beautiful and cuddly
And it's really good when you have two
And they are always there
When you need them most.

There are dogs, cats, rabbits,
Hamsters, goldfish and mice
As you can see there is more than one kind of pet
But this is as good as it gets!

Danielle Loughran (10)
St Mary's Primary School, Hamilton

Maths

M ental maths is magically mince,
A bsolutely boring too,
T erribly tiring as well,
H ated by everyone,
S uper duper rubbish.

Vincent Linden (9)
St Mary's Primary School, Hamilton

I Want To Be A Ballerina

I want to be a ballerina
Just like Princess Thumbelina.
And when I grow very tall
I'll quit school and do it all.
The boss came round putting paint on our nose
But I said, 'I would rather have it on my toes.'
On the stage I was nervous
Because I thought I would break my pelvis.
When I just turned sixteen
I became the dancing queen.
Sitting still in the pool
Thinking I should have stayed at school.

Maria Linden (10)
St Mary's Primary School, Hamilton

Fitba!

O fitba, fitba the beautiful game.
Aw the players that are great are very hard to tame.
Fay Thiery Henry to Ronaldinho, yey always hear fans chantin'
'Here we go! Here we go!'

I love playin' with the ball,
While guys are watchin' TV in the pub, drinking alcohol.

Maradonna and Pele are the best,
Trying to beat them?
Now that's a test.

Michael Lowe (10)
St Mary's Primary School, Hamilton

The Park

The park is a great place to play
Hide-and-seek every day.
With lots of trees to hide behind
And lots of fences to be climbed.
Come rain or shine
You'll find us there,
Playing all day without a care!
Till one day we saw a sign,
It said, 'No ball games or you'll get a fine'.
'That's okay with us,' we said,
'Because we'll play hide-and-seek
Till it's time for bed.'

Fraser Hamilton (10)
St Mary's Primary School, Hamilton

New York

I have been to New York,
Where nobody seems to sleep.
At night in the streets,
All the people you can meet,
Bright lights and loud music
Never ever stops,
And then you can go
And grab a bite to eat
Or perhaps a treat
Before you take in a show.

Gabrielle Aitchison (10)
St Mary's Primary School, Hamilton

Friends

My favourite show ever on TV has to be Friends,
It made me laugh right from the start, until the very end.
Those five crazy pals from downtown New York,
Monica was a nutter, Ross was a dork.
Phoebe was a weirdo, Chandler a clown,
Joey not too bright, Rachel a girl about town.
They sat in Central Park for a coffee and a chat,
Or just hung about in Monica's massive, trendy flat.
Joey was my favourite, he always made me laugh,
He was extremely cute, but absolutely daft.
But after one hundred and fifty episodes, it all had to come to an end,
So I watch them all on DVD again and again.

Amy Sullivan (10)
St Mary's Primary School, Hamilton

The Monster In The Cupboard

There's a monster in my cupboard
He gives me quite a scare.
Although I haven't seen him
It doesn't mean he isn't there.

I've imagined what he looks like
He is hairy and he is green.
His red eye is big and bulging
It makes him look quite mean.

One night I heard a roaring noise
When I slept in my bed.
I said to myself, 'Forget about it,'
And rested my sleepy head.

Nicholas Gallacher (11)
St Mary's Primary School, Hamilton

Anger

Anger is red like an erupting volcano
It sounds like a bomb exploding in my head.
Anger is dark red like a blazing fire
It tastes like a bitter lemon in my mouth.

Anger smells like a tyre thrown on a bonfire
It looks like a raging tornado heading my way
And sucking everything in its path.

When I think of anger I think of the time when
I crossed the road without waiting for my mum.
I could tell by looking at her that she was full of anger
As her face was very, very red!

Courtney Craig (10)
St Mary's Primary School, Hamilton

I Love My Dog Millie

I love my little Millie
She really is so silly
She is white and small
And plays all day with her ball
When I come home from school
She really plays the fool.

I love her with all my heart
And I hope we'll never part
Her eyes are black and bright
And she loves me with all her might.
Sometimes she gets me mad and yet
She is my favourite and loving pet!

Meghann Farrell (10)
St Mary's Primary School, Hamilton

Anger

Anger is red like an exploding volcano
with burning rocks coming out and lava leaking out.

Anger sounds like a stampede running through Glasgow
destroying everything in its path.

Anger tastes like a red-hot chilli pepper
with five different Indian spices on it.

Anger smells like a stink bomb made out of
old fish.

Anger looks like a T-rex eating a helpless
herbivore.

Anger reminds me of a man with his eyes out of
his sockets and big, scary, purple veins.

Callum Creechan (10)
St Mary's Primary School, Hamilton

At The Funfair

At the funfair
The log flumes go splish-splash,
While the roller coaster is very fast.
The dodgems go here and there
And the smell of candyfloss is in the air.
The big wheel goes round and round
And there are lots of sounds.
Screaming, shouting, laughter and fun,
It's the perfect place for everyone.
The carousel goes round a bend
And this is where my poem ends.

Alison Brophy (10)
St Mary's Primary School, Hamilton

Christmas

Christmas isn't Christmas till you've been told
go out and buy presents for all,
bake pies for them grannies
and help stir soup for your nanny.

Christmas is full of happiness
when kids are having fun
and adults are chilling out.

Then when Christmas ends
decorations go down
and children go back to school with a frown.
The fridge is empty and cupboards are bare
but I can't wait to do it all again next year.

Alison Tougher (10)
St Mary's Primary School, Hamilton

Pizza

I heat you up in the oven,
I take you out with care
And place you on the table.
Oh pizza you look so nice,
With toppings I desire,
Melting cheese and red hot sauce,
Your makers I admire.
I slice you into quarters
And serve you to my friends
You taste a treat and make a feast
Oh pizza you are great to eat.

Dario Palazzo (10)
St Mary's Primary School, Hamilton

Happiness

Happiness is yellow like the bright morning sun,
somewhere hot and somewhere fun.
Happiness sounds like children's laughter in the park,
not a fierce bulldog's bark.
Happiness looks like popcorn, hot dogs, chocolate
and fluffy pink candyfloss at the fair.
Happiness smells like a beautiful scented bouquet
of bright yellow roses in the summertime.
Happiness looks like big, beautiful, tall, yellow sunflowers
in a huge field.
Happiness reminds me of a beautiful, peaceful field
in the countryside down in Yorkshire.

Clare Kerr (10)
St Mary's Primary School, Hamilton

Anger

Anger is the colour
of a red, burning fire.

Anger sounds like elephants
rumbling through a jungle.

Anger looks like billowing black smoke
coming out of your ears.

Anger tastes like burning, hot peppers
sizzling in your mouth.

Anger reminds you of your brother or sister
annoying you.

Stephanie Robb (9)
St Mary's Primary School, Hamilton

Flowers

Flowers make me happy
From tiny seeds they grow
Flowers shine like sunlight on my life
I see them everywhere
From Scotland, England and Wales
I like to plant bulbs in spring
And watch the hyacinths grow
Flowers are beautiful
I don't know what I would do
Without flowers.

Amanda McInally (10)
St Mary's Primary School, Hamilton

I Love You Mum

Hearts of love are red,
'I love you Mum,' I said.
I gave her lovely fresh flowers
And smiled for hours and hours.

Close your eyes and dream,
Think of chocolate mint ice cream.
I wake with a morning kiss,
From Mum, who I always miss.

Kieran McGinnes (10)
St Mary's Primary School, Hamilton

Dads

D ads are great
A nd always there
D ads are special they
S uper care.

Sarah Aitchison (9)
St Mary's Primary School, Hamilton

My Dog

My dog Belle is barking mad!
She is always happy and never sad.
She likes to chase cats and squirrels too,
If you lift up her toy, she will play with you.
She likes nothing better than a big, long walk,
Followed by a juicy bone, for her alone.
She'll come in for tea
And put her paw on your knee.
She's cute and cuddly
And she'll do for me!

Megan Finnigan (10)
St Mary's Primary School, Hamilton

Hate

Hate is red like a raging bush fire,
Hate sounds like a stampede of animals,
Hate tastes like a spicy noodle,
Hate smells like a fire burning,
Hate reminds me of my big brother chasing me.

Christopher Murray (10)
St Mary's Primary School, Hamilton

Pets

P ets are lovely and cuddly
E verything in your life
T hey are always in your heart
S omething that is always there to talk to.

Alissa McGuigan (9)
St Mary's Primary School, Hamilton

Pets

My favourite pet is a dog,
they are friendly and fast.
Though I'd rather have a frog,
then a spell I'd cast.

I don't like bats,
They are black and creepy.
I would prefer a cat,
they are sly and sneaky.

Tigers are proud,
they are big and stripy.
Lions are loud,
then I see them go, 'Crikey.'

I love monkeys,
they are clever and fun.
I also like donkeys,
on the beach they run.

I have a pet called Fudge,
he is clever and blue.
He is a budgie
and he belongs to Ruth too.

Connor McEwan (9)
St Mary's Primary School, Lanark

My Two Cats

I have two cats
Neither are very fat
One called Clover,
One called Honey,
Both are funny
But didn't cost much money.
Eating, drinking, out to play,
They can be away all day.

Stephen Hilland (9)
St Mary's Primary School, Lanark

When I Am Older

When I am older
It'll be so great.
I could eat sweets all day
And go out at night.
I could go to the movies
I could go out for tea
I could go shopping for only me!
I could walk up Mount Everest
I could swim five miles
I could dance around America
The people would go wild!
I could swing on vines
Or shoot into space
I could play with my rabbits
And make them race!

But it won't be that brill
because I'll have to pay bills.
I'll get a cool job
but it'll still be boring.
I can't just sit around all day and play
I can't play tig in the park
I might forget my old friends too!
There's one thing I won't forget
It's my younger life
My younger life is fine.
I will stay with my younger life for now.

Rebecca Scott (10)
St Mary's Primary School, Lanark

When I'm Older

When I'm older
it'll be so great,
I'll sing and I'll dance
and I won't clean the plates.
I won't make my bed
and I won't eat my greens,
I'll have my own house
and I won't keep it clean.
I'll have my own cinema
and I'll have my own pool
and I'll have a flashy car
to drive the children to school.

The bad thing about it is
I'll have to pay the bills
and I'll have to get down on my knees
and clean up the spills
and when I look in the mirror
I'll have bags under my eyes
Then my husband will come in
and he'll jump and he'll sigh.

So maybe I'll just enjoy being young
and I might make it through
(if I just watch my tongue!)

Danielle Stewart (10)
St Mary's Primary School, Lanark

My Pet Holly The Cat

I have a cat called Holly
Who is very jolly
She came to stay on Christmas Day
And I shouted, 'Hip hip hooray.'

Sarah McQuoney (9)
St Mary's Primary School, Lanark

But . . .

When I'm older it will be so great
I'll blast right into space
or become an actor or presenter
well who cares? A celebrity.
I'll become rich
have five children
I won't clean the dishes and plates.

But . . .

I'll probably be scared to blast-off into space
there's a very slight chance I'll become a celebrity
I'll have to have a good job to become rich
I'll be bored stiff because I won't have anything to do!

Callum Johnstone (10)
St Mary's Primary School, Lanark

When I'm Older

When I'm older
It'll be so great
I will have a pint or two
I will go home and stay up till two
And that is what I will do

But when I'm older
It won't be so great
I will have a job
And I'll have to listen to my boss
I can't stay up late
But best of all I don't have to go to school

I will stay ten for now.

Christopher Cunningham (10)
St Mary's Primary School, Lanark

When I Am Older

When I am older
it'll be so cool
I will have a trampoline
and my own swimming pool.
I can stay up really late
and eat sweets all day
oh it'll be so great.

But when I am older
it won't be so great
'Cause there has to be a day
when I turn 58
and when I am sitting
watching a movie,
the bills come in
it won't be so groovy.

So I think I'll just stay eleven for now.

Ainsley Stark (11)
St Mary's Primary School, Lanark

When I'm Older

When I'm older it'll be so great
I'll build and build until my arms ache
I'll watch movies into the night
Cos nothing will be too old for me
I'll get a Ford GT
And do it up so much it'll be the best on the road.

But when I'm older
It won't be so great
I'll have to save money
I'll have to get a job
And get up early for it
I'll have to look after the kids.

So I'll just be the age that I am.

Kenneth Craig (10)
St Mary's Primary School, Lanark

Ten Going On Twenty

When I'm older . . .
it will be so great
I'll go over my garden gate
to the United States.
It's so good I feel like
baking a cake.
Now I'll go round my mates
to bake the cake
yippee! It's so great.

When I'm older . . .
it won't be so great
I'll have to wash the dishes
and clean the plates.
Sometimes I wish
I could dive in a
swimming pool
but I can't do that
so I'll just stay ten for now.

Roseanna Johnstone (10)
St Mary's Primary School, Lanark

When I'm Older

When I'm older
It'll be so great
I'll eat sweets all day long
And I'll dance to my favourite song.

But when I'm older
It won't be so great
Bills to pay, money to lose
I'll end up feeding the cows
So maybe eleven is great to be.

Chloe Lamarra (11)
St Mary's Primary School, Lanark

When I'm Older

When I'm older It'll be so great
I can eat pizzas and stay up late.
I'll have a mansion and a pool
Plus I won't have to go to school.
I'll buy every pair of shoes that look pretty
I'll go to art college and university.
I'll have servants to cook and clean
I'll be even richer than the Queen!

Although it won't all be frills
I'll need to buy my house and pay the bills.
My phone bill will be massive too
And I like expensive shoes.
Oh and I can't be a slob
I'll need to go out and get a job.

But I'm only a little girl
And I wouldn't change that for the world.

Esmée Gallagher (10)
St Mary's Primary School, Lanark

When I'm Older

When I'm older
it'll be so great
I'll run about
and lick all the plates
and fly to the United States
it'll be great!

But when I'm older
it might not be so great
I'll have to work
and have to pay
and I might have a *boring* day
so today I'll just stay
ten!

Gregor Frame (10)
St Mary's Primary School, Lanark

When I'm Older

When I'm older
It'll be so great
I'll go abroad to the United States
Then I'll move to London
Downing Street, number eight
I'll drive a posh car
Perhaps a Jaguar
My credit card will go swipe, swipe, swipe
I've just realised something
Oh cripes!

When I'm older
It won't be so great
All the bills to pay
It could end in dismay
They could take away my car
If I avoid MOT by far
If I get kicked out my house,
How will I live?
Maybe I'll stay eleven for now!

Helena Davidson (10)
St Mary's Primary School, Lanark

When I'm Older

When I'm older
it'll be so great
I'll have a pet snake
his name will be Drake
we'll play games and bake

but I'll have to pay the phone bill,
the tax for the house.
I'll have to pay for the food,
have to get a job.
So it won't be all so great.

Scott Ellis (11)
St Mary's Primary School, Lanark

I'm Only Ten

When I'm older
it'll be so great.
I'll go down the high street with all my mates!
I'll stay up till ten at night
and I'll watch every film I've never seen!

But when I'm older
it won't be such fun
especially if I have a son.
I'll need a job
even if my boss is a snob
there'll be no more having girlie fun.
I'll have to get up early for work
and I don't know how!
So I'll just stay ten for now!

Nicole Sykes (10)
St Mary's Primary School, Lanark

When I'm Older

When I'm older
It'll be so great
I'll play football until it's dark
I'll kick the ball right up to the sky
I'll ride my bike until light
I'll go as far as the ball went.

But when I'm older
It won't be so great
I'll have to work
I'll have to pay the bills
I'll have to clean my living room.

I think I'll just stay ten for now!

Craig Bustard (10)
St Mary's Primary School, Lanark

Ten For Now

When I'm older
it will be so fine
I could stay up
until any time
I could eat pizza
all day long
I could play over and over
my favourite song.
When I'm older
I'll be a vet
set up a website on the net.

But, when I'm older
it won't be so swell
if I don't clean the house
it will start to smell
and also it won't be so fine
cos I'll leave for work at some unearthly time.
I might get sacked
I might get dumped
but most of all I might get thumped.

So there's the reason I think somehow
that I'll just stay ten for now.

Erin McLeod (10)
St Mary's Primary School, Lanark

Pet Poem

Their names are Tanya and Tammy,
who were taken away from their mammy.
They soon learnt to play,
mostly in the litter tray,
but I love them best,
when they snuggle into my chest,
at the end of a long, hard day.

Jamie Cooper (8)
St Mary's Primary School, Lanark

When I'm Older

When I'm older
It'll be great
I'll climb the Buckingham Palace gate
I'll meet a new mate called Kate
Then I'll move to Bathgate
Where I'll watch the boys skate!

But when I'm older
It won't be so great
I could fall off the Buckingham Palace gate
And break my shoulder blade
Or I might not meet a new mate called Kate
And if I do she might clean plates.
I might not get to Bathgate
Or worst of all I might be too late
To see the boys skate!

But while I'm still young
I'll stick to climbing the garden gate
And watching my cousin skate!

Lesley Simpson (10)
St Mary's Primary School, Lanark

My Mum

There is a special person in my life
Who is there the whole day through
She loves me and guides me in everything I do.
I will love her forever
As she will me
Sometimes the way I thank her
Is by making her a cup of tea.

Emma Shields (10)
Sacred Heart Primary School

The Haunted House

The haunted house is in an old street,
It's been abandoned for years and years.
One night I went in,
I was filled with dreadful fears.
The curtains were torn and dusty,
On the window sills were squashed, dead flies,
Then in the distance I heard terrifying cries.
I walked towards the noises
And to my surprise,
A vampire jumped from hiding,
With fire in his eyes.
He looked at me grinning,
I could sense something was wrong,
I wish I was out of here,
I wish I was gone!
I ran rapidly to the door,
My heart was thumping more and more.
I just couldn't make it,
I was filled with great fright,
As he grabbed my neck, about to take a bite.
I woke up urgently with a squeal,
'Thank goodness,' I sighed . . . 'that wasn't real!'

Shannon Gordon (10)
Sacred Heart Primary School

Who Is It?

Someone that I know is really, really great,
That person that I know is my best mate,
So if on your face there's a frown,
To her it's just a smile turned upside down.
Now it's up to you to decide
Which friend do I hide?

Alex Craig (10)
Sacred Heart Primary School

My Funny Friend

My friend is funny,
She acts like a bunny,
She tells funny jokes
And makes people boke.
My friend is the best I've ever had,
Even though sometimes she is mad.
We share secrets together
And we never fall out.
We are best friends
And that's without a doubt.

Gemma Nicol (10)
Sacred Heart Primary School

My Teacher

M iss Cochrane,
Y es! She's the best,

T ruly the most special one yet,
E xtraordinary, fantastic,
A mazing at being herself,
C aring about her pupils,
H er hair is silky and soft,
E verlasting smile,
R are to find a better teacher than her.

Chelsea Porter (10)
Sacred Heart Primary School

Gran

I've often asked the angels
If they would from time to time,
Keep a watchful eye
On the gran that I call mine,
I know they pay you visits
But you'll never guess they are there,
They sprinkle magic dust on you,
It's called our angel care,
Don't ever feel alone Gran,
The angels are always there,
They're in the air above your head,
Telling you that I care.

Melissa Dougan (10)
Sacred Heart Primary School

The Secret Jaguar

My Jaguar is black,
That's a fact,
It is so cool,
People think I rule the school.
My car is black
And has got a soft roof,
It is even waterproof.
People call my car the 'Bull',
When I go to school,
People shout, 'Go! Go! Bull.'

Gary McAlpine (10)
Sacred Heart Primary School

The Fidgety Finches

It's cold today,
The finches are freezing!
They're sitting on our tree,
Looking in our window,
Fidget, fidget, fidget!

Where are our peanuts?
Where are our breadcrumbs?
Fidget, fidget, fidget!

Where's our fatty rind?
Where's our seeds?
Fidget, fidget, fidget!

Oh! Here he comes!
I wish he would stop whistling.
I think he's got a sore throat!
Fidget, fidget, fidget!

Throw us some peanuts!
Great, last night's pasta!
Oh! There's some buttery crusts.
Fidget, fidget, fidget!

Hurry up and eat!
Before the sparrows come,
Before the starlings come,
Before the crows come,
Yum, yum, yum!

Abbie Sloan (10)
Sacred Heart Primary School

The First And Worst Day At A Victorian School

I'm walking through the gates of school,
I'm wondering if the teachers will be cruel.
The teacher stamps right through the playground,
She really makes my stomach go round.
Then I walk into the class,
It has a lampshade made of brass.
The air in the class is really cold
And the rules on the wall are written in bold.
Then we are given a written test,
It looks really hard so I try my best.
Someone says, 'But,'
And she does her nut.
I am about to melt
And next thing I get the belt.
We go out to play,
I make a friend called May.
Then the bell goes,
We walk home in rows.

Hannah Victoria Black (10)
Woodhead Primary School

A Day In The Life Of A Victorian Child At School

I hear a lot of sounds like the belt or ruler,
When I'm in the Victorian school it sounds like a door getting slammed.

I saw a little boy getting the belt because he fell asleep
Because he was tired.

The teachers need to learn that children have feelings too.
I felt really sad when I saw the little boy getting hit
With the belt and so would you!

Andrew McDougall (10)
Woodhead Primary School

Christmas Signs

(Inspired by 'Snow' by Margaret R Moore)

Frigidly frost and foggy, the North Pole,
It hides Santa's workshop
And mischievous elves
And a magical sleigh
And chatters to the world,
Santa's on his way!

Kingly proud and colourful the tree
It sits in the corner
And traps lots of presents underneath
And lashings of decorations
And yells out
'Merry Christmas!'

Jordan Roy (11)
Woodhead Primary School

Signs Of Christmas

(Inspired by 'Snow' by Margaret R Moore)

Gleaming, glowing and luminous the lights;
They decorate the tree
And cling to windows
And drape over gardens
And sing to the world
Darkness no more!

Twinkling, glittering and dazzling the stars
They hang from the clouds
And rest on the moon
And release the snowflakes from the sky
And murmur to the world,
'Jesus is born!'

Kimberley Fleming (11)
Woodhead Primary School

David Livingstone

He looked like an old foggy film,
He smelt like an old chestnut rotting away,
He sounded as if he was a really nice man
But he didn't look like it at all.

His clothes smelt and felt like old raw cotton
And his shoes were as brown as a sty,
His voice was as deep as a lion's roar,
His hands were all dirty and his eyes were all bloodshot,
I just had to ask him what he did in Africa
And about all the good things he'd done.
I was kind of scared when I saw him at first
But he's a really nice man,
He'll do you no harm.

Taylor Jeffrey (10)
Woodhead Primary School

Florence's Fabulous Poem

Walking down the corridor,
It was deep and dark,
Taking care of all the men who were in the war.
Diseases flying round the hospital like a dragonfly,
All the men crying because they were wounded.
Shining bright like a light,
Speaking kind words for all who heard.

Kirsty Craig (10)
Woodhead Primary School

The Schoolboy

Teachers shouting loud and clear,
'Get back in your seat!'
Hopefully I won't get the belt,
If only I got a couple of sweets.
The classroom is basic black, grey and white
And maybe if you add some colour
You would get the decoration right!

The gym hall's really boring
And so is the kitchen too!
And if you add some decent stuff
We would learn something too!
We would learn how to run and jump
And learn some manners too.
So why don't you listen to me
Because then we wouldn't reek of stew.

By the way my name's Stuart,
I hate maths and English too.
Is your school the same as ours?
Well maybe you have a decent school!

Stuart Macdonald (10)
Woodhead Primary School

David Livingstone

He was born in 1813
On March 19th.
David went to Africa
Exploring for thirty years,
Telling people about God,
Saying that God was beside them.
He was leaving Africa
And nearly got attacked by a lion.
David died in 1873.
He died when he was praying
Next to his bed.

Scott Jannaway (10)
Woodhead Primary School

David Livingstone

He was born on March 19th
In Blantyre, that is where
David went to Africa
He did it to spread the word
Of Jesus Christ the Lord
And the maker of Earth, God.

David was attacked by a lion
When he was in the wilderness
He discovered Victoria Falls
And lots of plants and animals
David published a book
'Missionary Travels' it was called.

He died in 1873
And was buried in Westminster Abbey
There is a statue of David Livingstone
In Glasgow, quite near his home
And that's the end of Livingstone
The famous Victorian.

Cameron Humphreys (10)
Woodhead Primary School

Working Hard

Working day and night for little money
The smells of dried blood on the floor
The cotton mills going click-clack
People tired of working all night
If they don't finish the work they will get the belt
People falling asleep in the mill
And hurting their arms and fingers
Hearing the sound of screams
When arms and fingers get trapped in the mill
Hungry children want food.

Jennifer Gray (10)
Woodhead Primary School

It's Hard To Be A Maid

It's hard to be a maid,
Getting up early in the morning,
Working all day cleaning,
Masters telling you what to do.

Once a day I change the coal,
It smells of smoke, it's rough and sooty too.
I work in the scullery twice a week
And a nursery to sweep,
It's hard to be a maid.

I set the table every night,
So tired, so hungry,
We make the dinner,
The masters eat it up,
It's hard to be a maid.

We go to sleep at 10 o'clock,
I fall asleep so quickly,
After a long day of work,
It's hard to be a maid.

Allison Day (10)
Woodhead Primary School

Victorian Mill

At the old mill
Lots of crime and slime
Cries of pain in the mill
Blood and accidents all the time
There's Mr Pip with his whip
Coming to hit all the time
The smell of smoke
Clitter-clatter, pitter-patter
Tired children all sleepy too
With long hours and such low pay,
Two pence a day.

Fraser McEwan (10)
Woodhead Primary School

In A Victorian School

Today I am in deep trouble,
I made little John bubble,
He is really a pain,
So I called him insane
And he told Mr Charlie on me.
Mr Charlie looked at me fiercely,
He pulled my arm and said, 'Come,'
I looked little John in the eyes,
I thought that I should have told lies,
But it's far too late for that now.
Mr Charlie got out the long belt,
You didn't know how bad I felt,
He told me to hold out my hands,
So I did what I was told right away,
Mr Charlie he hit me and I stopped
And then I cried out a very loud 'Oouch'.
Well that's Victorian schools for you,
You wouldn't want to go back then,
I hope I don't get that belt again
Because it's very sore, I tell you *it's sore*.

Laura Garvin (10)
Woodhead Primary School

Chimney Sweep

I got stuck up the chimney
They had to pull me out
Nearly couldn't breathe
I slipped but just stopped in time
For I was two inches away from the fireplace
Which I thought would be my grave
I had to climb back up
Shaking in fear
I made it
To fight for what tomorrow would bring.

Hazel Connolly (10)
Woodhead Primary School

The Lady Of The Lamp

Walking slowly round weary heads
Lying on small freezing beds
All around so quick and quiet
Suddenly a scream is heard
Someone dying in the room
Finding someone facing doom

Pacing tiredly with a lamp
Watch your step, it's surely damp
Everyone asleep
Fighting in the deep,
Deep sleep
It's the lady of the shining bright light.

Mary-Jo Getliffe (10)
Woodhead Primary School